Better Homes and Gardens

FARMER'S MARKET

COOK BOOK

BETTER HOMES AND GARDENS BOOKS
Des Moines

WE CARE!

All of us at Better Homes and Gardens® Books are dedicated to providing you with the information and ideas you need to create tasty foods. We welcome your comments and suggestions. Write us at: Better Homes and Gardens® Books, Cookbook Editorial Department, BB-117, 1716 Locust St., Des Moines, IA 50309-3023

If you would like to order additional copies of any of our books, call 1-800-678-2803 or check with your local bookstore.

FARMER'S MARKET COOK BOOK

Writers: Linda Henry, Heidi Kaisand
Graphic Designer: Lynda Haupert
Project Manager: Jennifer Darling
Copy Editor: Jennifer Mitchell
Test Kitchen Product Supervisor: Marilyn Cornelius
Food Stylists: Janet Herwig, Mable Hoffman
Food Photographers: Peter Krumhardt, Perry Struse, Joan Vanderschuit
Illustrations: Lynda Haupert

BETTER HOMES AND GARDENS® BOOKS
An Imprint of Meredith® Books

President, Book Group: Joseph J. Ward
Vice President and Editorial Director: Elizabeth P. Rice
Executive Editor: Connie Schrader
Art Director: Ernest Shelton
Prepress Production Manager: Randall Yontz
Production Editor: Paula Forest
Test Kitchen Director: Sharon Stilwell

On the cover: Yellow Pepper and Red Tomato Salad

Our seal assures you that every recipe in the *Farmer's Market Cook Book* has been tested in the Better Homes and Gardens® Test Kitchen. This means that each recipe is practical and reliable, and meets our high standards of taste appeal. We guarantee your satisfaction with this book for as long as you own it.

*A*ll across the U.S., farmer's markets are alive and thriving—in big cities and rural communities alike. From huge permanent structures, to pickup tailgates in a shopping mall parking lot, to card tables set up around a town square, today's farmer's markets are as varied as America's countryside. But all the markets have one thing in common—a profusion of fresh-from-the-farm produce.

When the early, wet and warm days of spring arrive, we look forward to the first crops appearing at the local farmer's markets—asparagus and rhubarb. Then comes summer—the hot days and warm nights give us juicy, plump tomatoes, tart, red cherries, rosy plums, snowy white cauliflower, and snappy green beans. And finally, as the fall harvest approaches, we get deeply-colored apples and pears, crisp turnips, and a rainbow of hard-shell squash.

But what do you do when you go overboard and arrive home from your farmer's market with more broccoli, zucchini, and berries than you can possibly use? That's where *Better Homes and Gardens® Farmer's Market Cook Book* comes in. This book is filled with delicious answers to that question. How do Broccoli-Chèvre Soufflé, Sautéed Zucchini and Apples, and Blackberry Swirl Cheesecake sound? Or maybe Oriental Broccoli Stir-Fry, Zucchini Chocolate Cake, or Fresh Raspberry Mousse? Whether you're rediscovering an old favorite, or getting acquainted with some new and unusual garden goodies, you'll enjoy them all in the dishes on these pages.

So head on out to the closest farmer's market and do some shopping in the sunshine. Don't know where to find one? Check your local newspaper or contact your local chamber of commerce, state department of agriculture, or county extension office.

Contents

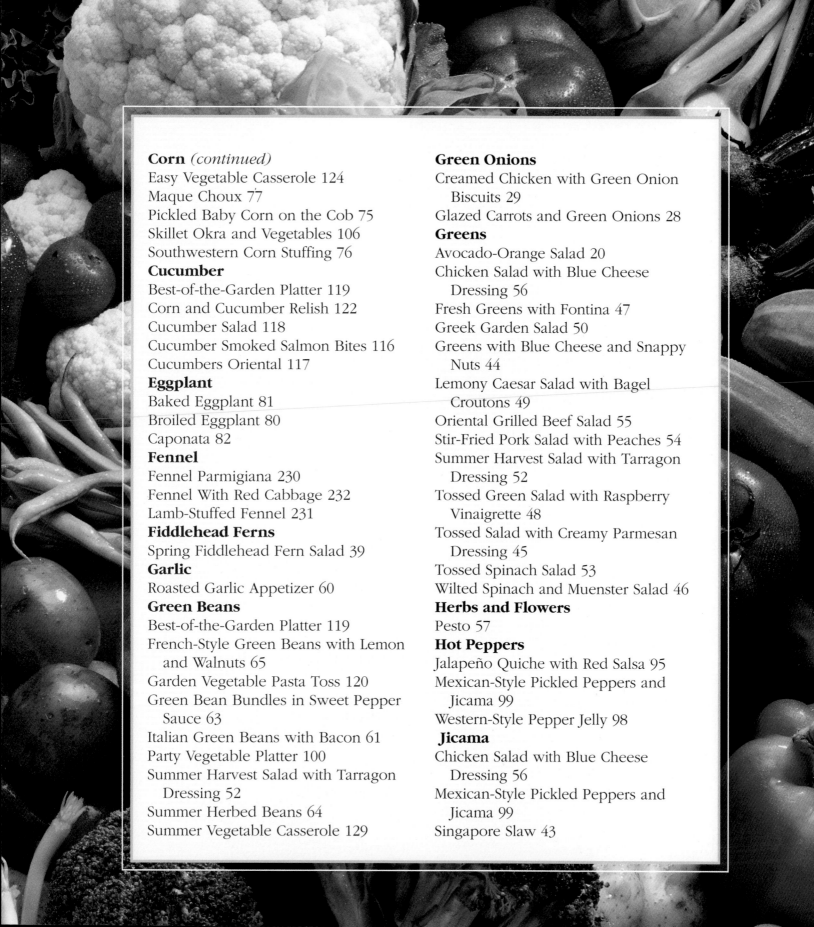

ASPARAGUS

Rainbow Garden Toss

Makes 4 servings

To keep asparagus fresh, wrap the bases of the spears in wet paper towels and keep them tightly sealed in a plastic bag. Refrigerate for up to 4 days.

1 pound asparagus, bias sliced into 1-inch pieces (3 cups)
1 medium carrot, cut into julienne strips (½ cup)
1 small yellow summer squash or zucchini, halved lengthwise and sliced ¼ inch thick (1 cup)

▼
4 teaspoons lemon juice
1 tablespoon margarine or butter, melted
1 tablespoon snipped fresh dill or 1 teaspoon dried dillweed
¼ teaspoon salt

Per Serving

Calories	56
Protein	2 g
Carbohydrate	6 g
Total Fat	3 g
Saturated Fat	1 g
Cholesterol	0 mg
Sodium	181 mg
Potassium	301 mg

Place a steamer basket in a saucepan. Add water to just below the bottom of the steamer basket. Bring to boiling. Add asparagus and carrots. Cover and reduce heat. Steam for 5 minutes. Add yellow summer squash or zucchini. Steam for 4 to 5 minutes more or till crisp-tender. Transfer to a serving bowl. ▼ **Meanwhile,** combine the lemon juice, melted margarine or butter, dill, and salt. Pour over the vegetables and toss lightly.

ASPARAGUS

Asparagus with Citrus Mock Hollandaise

Makes 6 to 8 servings

Per serving

Calories	105
Protein	2 g
Carbohydrate	4 g
Total Fat	10 g
Saturated Fat	2 g
Cholesterol	10 mg
Sodium	61 mg.
Potassium	238 m

2 **pounds asparagus spears**
▼
¼ **cup dairy sour cream**
¼ **cup mayonnaise or salad dressing**

½ **teaspoon finely shredded lemon peel**
1 **teaspoon lemon juice**
   Milk
   Lemon peel strips (optional)

Tender, green, and crisp— spring's signature vegetable needs nothing more than a light and lemony sauce. "Mock" means it sidesteps traditional egg yolks in favor of a mayonnaise shortcut.

Break off woody asparagus where spears snap easily; scrape off scales. Wash asparagus. Place a steamer basket in a saucepan. Add water to just below the bottom of the steamer basket. Bring to boiling. Add asparagus. Cover and reduce heat. Steam for 4 to 8 minutes or till crisp-tender. ▼ **Meanwhile,** for sauce, in a small saucepan combine sour cream, mayonnaise or salad dressing, lemon peel, and lemon juice. Stir in enough milk (1 to 2 teaspoons) to make of desired consistency. Cook and stir over low heat till heated through, but *do not boil.* Serve over asparagus. Garnish with lemon peel strips, if desired.

Asparagus-Orange Stir-Fry

Makes 4 servings

When you're cleaning asparagus stalks, remove the scales with a vegetable peeler, if you like.

½ to 1 teaspoon finely shredded orange peel
¼ cup orange juice
¼ cup water
2 teaspoons honey
1½ teaspoons cornstarch
½ teaspoon toasted sesame oil

▼

1 tablespoon cooking oil
1 pound asparagus, cut into 2-inch pieces (4 cups)
1 medium orange, peeled and sectioned
2 teaspoons toasted sesame seeds

Per serving

Calories	84
Protein	3 g
Carbohydrate	9 g
Total Fat	5 g
Saturated Fat	1 g
Cholesterol	0 mg
Sodium	4 mg
Potassium	284 mg

For sauce, in a small mixing bowl stir together the orange peel, orange juice, water, honey, cornstarch, and toasted sesame oil. Set aside.
▼ **Pour cooking oil** into a wok or a large skillet. (Add more oil as necessary during cooking.) Preheat over medium-high heat. Add asparagus; stir-fry for 4 to 5 minutes or till asparagus is crisp-tender. Push asparagus from center of the wok or the skillet. Stir the sauce and add it to the center of the wok or the skillet. Cook and stir till thickened and bubbly. Stir asparagus into sauce to coat. Gently stir in the orange sections. Transfer to serving platter. Sprinkle with sesame seeds.

RHUBARB

Whole Wheat-Rhubarb Pudding Cake

Makes 8 to 10 servings

5 cups sliced rhubarb
¼ cup sugar
▼
1¼ cups all-purpose flour
1 cup sugar
½ cup whole wheat flour
½ cup chopped pecans
1¼ teaspoons baking powder
½ teaspoon ground cinnamon

¼ teaspoon salt
⅛ teaspoon ground nutmeg
¾ cup milk
¼ cup margarine or butter, melted
▼
1¼ cups sugar
1 tablespoon cornstarch
1¼ cups boiling water
▼
Whipped cream (optional)

Come January, pull out the rhubarb you stashed in the freezer last spring and make this homey dessert. Let the frozen fruit stand for 15 or 20 minutes or till it's partially thawed but still icy.

Place the sliced rhubarb in a 13x9x2-inch baking dish. Sprinkle the ¼ cup sugar over the rhubarb. ▼ **In a medium mixing bowl** stir together the all-purpose flour, the 1 cup sugar, whole wheat flour, chopped pecans, baking powder, cinnamon, salt, and nutmeg. Add the milk and melted margarine or butter. Stir till combined. Spoon the batter over the rhubarb and spread evenly. ▼ **In a medium mixing bowl** stir together the 1¼ cups sugar and the cornstarch. Add the boiling water and stir till sugar dissolves. Slowly pour the mixture over the top of the batter. ▼ **Bake** in a 375° oven about 45 minutes or till top tests done. (To prevent overbrowning, cover the dish for the last 10 minutes, if necessary.) Let cool for 30 minutes. Serve with whipped cream, if desired.

Rhubarb Slush

Makes 12 servings

Perfect for a bridal shower punch! Pour the mixture into a punch bowl and add the carbonated beverage.

3 cups rhubarb cut into
   ½-inch pieces (1 pound)
1 cup water
⅓ cup sugar
▼
1 cup vodka *or* apple juice
1 6-ounce can frozen pink
   lemonade concentrate,
   thawed

▼
1 1-liter bottle lemon-lime
   carbonated beverage
   Fresh mint (optional)

Per serving

Calories	131
Protein	0 g
Carbohydrate	23 g
Total Fat	0 g
Saturated Fat	0 g
Cholesterol	0 mg
Sodium	12 mg
Potassium	99 mg

In a large saucepan combine rhubarb, water, and sugar. Bring to boiling. Reduce heat; cover and simmer 5 minutes or till rhubarb is tender. Cool slightly. ▼ **Pour half of the mixture** into a blender container or food processor bowl. Cover and blend or process till smooth. Pour into a medium bowl. Repeat with remaining rhubarb mixture. Stir in vodka or apple juice and lemonade concentrate. Pour into an 8x8x2-inch baking pan. Cover and freeze for several hours or till firm. ▼ **Before serving,** let rhubarb mixture made with apple juice stand at room temperature for 45 minutes to thaw. (Rhubarb mixture made with vodka does not need to thaw.) To serve, scoop about ⅓ *cup* of the rhubarb mixture into each glass. Fill each glass with about ⅓ *cup* of the carbonated beverage. Top each serving with mint, if desired.

Artichokes Stuffed with Feta Cheese

Makes 4 servings

Per serving

Calories	200
Protein	7 g
Carbohydrate	24 g
Total Fat	10 g
Saturated Fat	3 g
Cholesterol	12 mg
Sodium	356 mg
Potassium	417 mg

2 **medium artichokes**
  (about 10 ounces each)
  Lemon juice
  ▼
3 **tablespoons lemon juice**
2 **tablespoons olive oil** *or*
  salad oil
1 **tablespoon water**
1 **tablespoon snipped fresh**
  oregano or ½ teaspoon
  dried oregano, crushed

  ▼
½ **cup bulgur**
¼ **teaspoon salt**
1 **large tomato, peeled,**
  seeded, and chopped
  (1¼ cups)
½ **cup crumbled feta cheese**
  (2 ounces)
¼ **cup snipped parsley**

Serve this first-course salad with a light red wine such as Beaujolais or a white wine such as chardonnay.

Wash artichokes; trim stems and remove loose outer leaves. Cut off 1 inch from each top; snip off the sharp leaf tips. Brush cut edges with a little lemon juice. ▼ **Place a steamer basket** in a large saucepan. Add water to just below the bottom of the steamer basket. Bring to boiling. Add artichokes. Cover and reduce heat. Steam for 20 to 25 minutes or till a leaf pulls out easily. Drain artichokes upside down on paper towels. When cool, halve each artichoke lengthwise. Pull out centerleaves and scrape out choke; discard choke Place artichoke halves in a plastic bag set in a deep bowl. ▼ **For marinade,** in a small mixing bowl combine the 3 tablespoons lemon juice, olive oil or salad oil, water, and oregano.Pour over artichokes in bag. Close bag and turn   artichokes to coat well. Marinate in the refrigerator for several hours,   turning bag occasionally. ▼ **Meanwhile,** in a medium mixing bowl combine bulgur, salt, and 1 cup *hot water*, let stand for 1 hour. Drain well, pressing out excess water. Combine the drained bulgur, chopped tomato, feta cheese, and parsley. Cover and chill thoroughly. ▼ **To serve,** drain artichokes, reserving marinade. Place artichoke halves, cut side up, on a serving platterof shredded lettuce. Stir marinade into bulgur mixture. Spoon some of the bulgur mixture into each artichoke half. Place any additional bulgur mixture in a bowl and serve with artichokes.

Artichokes
With Tarragon Cream
Makes 4 servings

To store fresh artichokes, place them in a plastic bag and refrigerate. They are best if used within a couple of days, but will keep for up to a week.

**4 medium artichokes
(about 10 ounces each)
Lemon juice**
▼
**3 green onions, chopped
(⅓ cup)
2 tablespoons water
1 8-ounce package
Neufchâtel cheese
2 tablespoons lemon juice
or lime juice**

**1 teaspoon snipped fresh
tarragon or ¼ teaspoon
dried tarragon, crushed
⅛ teaspoon pepper
¼ cup milk**
▼
**Lemon slices (optional)
Fresh tarragon (optional)**

Per serving

Calories	219
Protein	10 g
Carbohydrate	17 g
Total Fat	14 g
Saturated Fat	9 g
Cholesterol	45 mg
Sodium	348 mg
Potassium	537 mg

Wash artichokes; trim stems and remove loose outer leaves. Cut off 1 inch from each top; snip off the sharp leaf tips. Brush cut edges with a little lemon juice. ▼ **Place a steamer basket** in a large saucepan. Add water to just below the bottom of the steamer basket. Bring to boiling. Add artichokes. Cover and reduce heat. Steam for 20 to 25 minutes or till a leaf pulls out easily. Drain artichokes upside down on paper towels. Spread leaves apart. Pull out center leaves and scrape out choke with a spoon; discard choke. ▼ **For cream mixture,** in a small saucepan combine green onion and water. Cook, covered, for 1 to 2 minutes or till onion is tender. Drain. Add cheese; cook and stir over low heat about 1 minute or till cheese softens. Remove from heat; stir in the 2 tablespoons lemon juice or lime juice, tarragon, and pepper. Add the milk and stir till smooth. ▼ **Spoon cream mixture** into the center of each artichoke. Garnish with lemon slices and fresh tarragon, if desired. To eat, remove and dip leaves in the cream mixture.

AVOCADO

Chilled Avocado Soup

Makes 4 servings

Per Serving

Calories	196
Protein	7 g
Carbohydrate	10 g
Total Fat	15 g
Saturated Fat	3 g
Cholesterol	5 mg
Sodium	346 mg
Potassium	666 mg

2 **medium avocados, seeded, peeled and cut up**

1½ **cups chicken broth**

1 **8-ounce carton plain yogurt**

2 **tablespoons snipped fresh basil or 1 teaspoon**

dried basil, crushed

¼ **teaspoon pepper**

¼ **to ⅓ cup milk**

▼

2 **tablespoons finely chopped walnuts**

Spice up this soup by serving it with Snappy Nuts (see recipe, page 44) instead of the chopped walnuts.

In a blender container combine avocado, chicken broth, ¾ *cup* of the yogurt, basil, and pepper. Cover and blend till smooth. Stir in milk to desired consistency. Cover surface with plastic wrap. Chill up to 6 hours. ▼ **To serve,** ladle into soup bowls. Garnish with a dollop of the remaining yogurt and sprinkle with chopped walnuts.

AVOCADO

Avocado-Orange Salad

Makes 4 servings

Firm-ripe avocados are ideal for slicing. Refrigerate them and use within a few days.

2 tablespoons avocado oil *or* salad oil
2 tablespoons raspberry vinegar
2 teaspoons honey
½ teaspoon snipped fresh mint *or* pinch dried mint, crushed
▼
4 leaves red-tipped leaf lettuce

2 cups shredded red-tipped leaf lettuce
1 large avocado, seeded, peeled, and thinly sliced
2 medium oranges, peeled and sectioned
¼ cup red raspberries or sliced strawberries

Per Serving

Calories	173
Protein	2 g
Carbohydrate	12 g
Total Fat	15 g
Saturated Fat	2 g
Cholesterol	0 mg
Sodium	9 mg
Potassium	459 mg

For vinaigrette, in a screw-top jar combine avocado oil or salad oil, raspberry vinegar, honey, and mint. Cover and shake well. ▼ **Line 4 salad plates** with lettuce leaves. On each plate arrange shredded lettuce, avocado slices, orange sections, and raspberries or strawberries. Shake vinaigrette well; pour over each salad.

Nutrition Analysis

Keep track of your daily nutrition needs by using the information we provided at the end of each recipe. We've analyzed the nutrition content of each recipe serving for you. When a recipe gives an ingredient substitution, we used the first choice in the analysis. If it makes a range of servings (such as 4 to 6), we used the smallest number. Ingredients listed as optional weren't included in the calculations.

Sweet Pickled Beets

Makes 5 half-pints (20 servings)

Per Serving

Calories	52
Protein	1 g
Carbohydrate	14 g
Total Fat	0 g
Saturated Fat	0 g
Cholesterol	0 mg
Sodium	16 mg
Potassium	139 mg

2 pounds beets

▼

2 medium onions, thinly sliced
1⅓ cups vinegar
1 cup sugar
4 whole cloves

3 inches stick cinnamon, broken
1 teaspoon mustard seed
2 sprigs celery leaves
¼ teaspoon whole black peppercorns

An old-fashioned favorite that's finding new life with today's country cooks.

To cook beets, cut off all but 1 inch of stems and roots; wash. Do not peel. Cook, covered, in boiling, salted water for 40 to 50 minutes or till just tender. Drain; cool slightly. Slip skins off beets. Cut into ¼-inch-thick slices. ▼ **In a 4-quart Dutch oven** combine onions, vinegar, sugar, and ⅔ cup *water*. Tie cloves, cinnamon, mustard seed, celery leaves, and peppercorns in a 100 percent cotton cheesecloth bag. Add to vinegar mixture. Bring to boiling; reduce heat. Cover and simmer for 15 minutes. Discard bag. ▼ **Pack beets** into hot, *sterilized* half-pint jars. Pour onions and vinegar mixture over beets, leaving a ½-inch headspace. Wipe rims and adjust lids. Process in a boiling-water canner for 30 minutes. (Begin timing when water boils.)

BEETS

Orange-Beet Salad

Makes 4 servings

Besides its wonderful orange flavor, this salad gets a boost from toasted walnuts and walnut oil. Walnut oil is golden-colored with a pronounced nut flavor and rich aroma. Look for it at specialty shops and some larger supermarkets.

3 **medium beets
    (about ¾ pound)**
    ▼
3 **tablespoons walnut oil *or*
    salad oil**
1 **teaspoon shredded
    orange peel**
2 **tablepoons orange juice**
1 **tablespoon white wine
    vinegar *or* white vinegar**

▼
2 **tablespoons broken
    walnuts, toasted**
3 **tablespoons crumbled
    feta cheese**
¼ **teaspoon coarsely ground
    pepper**

Per Serving

Calories	149
Protein	2 g
Carbohydrate	6 g
Total Fat	14 g
Saturated Fat	2 g
Cholesterol	4 mg
Sodium	83 mg
Potassium	229 mg

To cook beets, cut off all but 1 inch of stems and roots; wash. Do not peel. Cook, covered, in boiling salted water for 40 to 50 minutes or till just tender. Drain; cool slightly. Slip skins off beets. Cut beets into ¼-inch-thick slices. (You should have 2 cups). ▼ **Meanwhile, for dressing,** in a screw-top jar combine walnut oil or salad oil, orange peel, orange juice, and vinegar. Cover and shake well. ▼ **In a medium mixing bowl** gently toss the beet slices with the dressing. Cover and chill for 2 to 24 hours. ▼ **To serve,** let mixture come to room temperature. Gently stir nuts into beets. Sprinkle with feta cheese and pepper. Serve with a slotted spoon.

EARLY CROP
BEETS

Creamed Beets
With Horseradish

Makes 4 servings

Per Serving

Calories	169
Protein	2 g
Carbohydrate	15 g
Total Fat	12 g
Saturated Fat	5 g
Cholesterol	13 mg
Sodium	430 mg
Potassium	328 mg

1 **pound beets**
   ▼
1 **small onion, chopped**
   (⅓ cup)
2 **tablespoons margarine** *or*
   butter
2 **tablespoons sugar**
1 **teaspoon cornstarch**

½ **teaspoon salt**
¼ **teaspoon pepper**
⅓ **cup water**
1 **tablespoon vinegar**
½ **cup dairy sour cream**
1 **tablespoon prepared**
   horseradish

Store unwashed fresh beets in an open plastic bag or a plastic bag with holes in it. The beets will last up to a week in the refrigerator.

To cook beets, cut off all but 1 inch of stems and roots; wash. Do not peel. Cook, covered, in boiling, salted water for 40 to 50 minutes or till just tender. Drain; cool slightly. Slip skins off beets. Cut beets into cubes. (You should have 2½ cups). ▼ **In the saucepan** cook onion in margarine or butter till onion is tender but not brown. Stir in the sugar, cornstarch, salt, and pepper. Stir in water and vinegar. Cook and stir over medium heat till thickened and bubbly. Add beets. Cook and stir for 2 minutes more. Reduce the heat. Stir in sour cream and horseradish. Heat through. *Do not boil.* Serve immediately.

CARROTS

Baby Carrots
With Pineapple Glaze

Makes 4 servings

Per Serving

Calories	116
Protein	2 g
Carbohydrate	28 g
Total Fat	0 g
Saturated Fat	0 g
Cholesterol	0 mg
Sodium	145 mg
Potassium	403 mg

1 **pound tiny whole carrots**
3 **medium leeks
    (12 ounces), sliced
    ½ inch thick (1 cup)**
    ▼
1 **cup unsweetened
    pineapple, orange, *or*
    apple juice**

2 **teaspoons cornstarch**
½ **teaspoon grated ginger-
    root or ⅛ teaspoon
    ground ginger**
⅛ **teaspoon salt**
⅛ **teaspoon ground nutmeg
    Plain yogurt (optional)**

This side dish goes together quickly because tiny whole carrots don't need to be peeled before cooking.

To trim carrots, leave 1 to 2 inches of stem; it is not necessary to peel them. In a medium saucepan cook carrots, covered, in a small amount of boiling water for 5 minutes. Add sliced leeks; cook about 5 minutes more or till carrots are crisp-tender. Drain and set aside. ▼ **For glaze,** in the same saucepan combine juice, cornstarch, gingerroot or ground ginger, salt, and nutmeg. Cook and stir over medium heat till thickened and bubbly. Cook and stir for 1 minute more. Stir in vegetables; heat through. Garnish each serving with a dollop of plain yogurt, if desired.

Buttermilk Carrot Cake

Makes 16 servings

Watching your calories? Then you had best opt for another dessert—this moist, heavy cake is loaded with them.

2 cups all-purpose flour
2 cups sugar
2 teaspoons baking soda
1½ teaspoons ground cinnamon
1 teaspoon baking powder
¼ teaspoon salt
4 medium carrots, shredded (2 cups)
¼ cup buttermilk or sour milk

¼ cup cooking oil
1 8¼-ounce can crushed pineapple, drained
1 cup chopped walnuts
3 eggs
½ cup coconut
1 teaspoon vanilla
▼
Buttermilk Glaze
Nutty Cream Cheese Frosting

Per Serving

Calories	538
Protein	6 g
Carbohydrate	77 g
Total Fat	25 g
Saturated Fat	6 g
Cholesterol	52 mg
Sodium	321 mg
Potassium	178 mg

Grease and lightly flour two 9x1½-inch round baking pans (or one 13x9x2-inch baking pan); set aside. In a large mixing bowl combine flour, sugar, baking soda, cinnamon, baking powder, and salt. Add shredded carrot, buttermilk or sour milk, cooking oil, pineapple, nuts, eggs, coconut, and vanilla. Stir till combined. Spread batter in prepared pans. ▼ **Bake** in a 350° oven for 40 to 45 minutes or till cakes spring back when touched lightly. Pour Buttermilk Glaze evenly over tops of cakes. Cool cakes in pans on wire racks for 15 minutes. Remove layer cakes from pans and place on wire racks (do not remove cake from 13x9x2-inch pan). Cool completely. Frost with Nutty Cream Cheese Frosting. Store in the refrigerator.

Buttermilk Glaze

In a medium saucepan combine ½ cup *sugar,* ¼ cup *buttermilk or sour milk,* ¼ cup *margarine or butter,* and 2 teaspoons *light corn syrup.* Bring to boiling; reduce heat. Cook and stir for 4 minutes. Remove from heat and stir in ½ teaspoon *vanilla.*

Nutty Cream Cheese Frosting

In a large mixing bowl beat two 3-ounce packages *cream cheese,* ½ cup softened *margarine or butter,* and 2 teaspoons *vanilla* with an electric mixer on medium to high speed till light and fluffy. Gradually add 4½ to 4¾ cups sifted *powdered sugar,* beating to spreading consistency. Stir in ½ cup chopped *walnuts.* Makes about 2 cups.

CARROTS

Carrot-Parsnip Mousse

Make 6 servings

Per Serving

Calories	143
Protein	6 g
Carbohydrate	17 g
Total Fat	6 g
Saturated Fat	1 g
Cholesterol	107 mg
Sodium	228 mg
Potassium	373 mg

1 **pound carrots (6 to 8 medium), thinly sliced**
½ **pound parsnips, coarsely chopped (1½ cups)**
▼
3 **eggs**
¼ **cup sour cream dip with chives**
1 **teaspoon finely shredded orange peel**

½ **teaspoon ground nutmeg**
¼ **teaspoon salt**
⅛ **teaspoon pepper**
▼
3 **tablespoons finely chopped almonds**
3 **tablespoons snipped parsley**
▼
Shredded zucchini (optional)

These individual molds of hot, pureed vegetables, with a whisper of orange-nutmeg sweetness, are a delightful accompaniment to baked ham.

In a large saucepan cook carrots and parsnips in a small amount of boiling water about 15 minutes or till very tender. Drain carrot-parsnip mixture. Remove 18 carrot slices; set aside. ▼ **In a blender** container or food processor bowl combine eggs, sour cream dip, orange peel, nutmeg, salt, and pepper. Add *half* of the carrot-parsnip mixture. Cover and blend or process till nearly smooth. Add remaining carrot-parsnip mixture. Cover and continue blending till smooth. ▼ **Toss together** the chopped almonds and parsley. Grease bottom and sides of six 6-ounce soufflé dishes or custard cups. Coat sides, not the bottoms, with the almond-parsley mixture. Use a small hors d'oeuvre cutter to make decorative cutouts from reserved carrot slices. Arrange 3 carrot cutouts on the bottom of each dish. Spoon carrot-parsnip mixture into dishes. Smooth top with a spatula. ▼ **Bake** in a 350° oven for 20 to 25 minutes or till a knife inserted near center comes out clean. Let stand 3 minutes. Run knife around edge. Unmold. Arrange on a platter lined with shredded zucchini, if desired.

CARROTS

Glazed Carrots And Green Onions

Makes 4 servings

Savor fresh carrots all year long by blanching tiny whole or cut-up carrots and freezing them for up to 1 year.

1 pound carrots (6 to 8 medium), roll-cut* (4 cups)

▼

4 green onions, bias sliced into 1- inch pieces (⅔ cup)

2 tablespoons honey
2 tablespoons margarine or butter
⅛ teaspoon ground ginger Pepper

Per Serving

Calories	132
Protein	1 g
Carbohydrate	20 g
Total Fat	6 g
Saturated Fat	1 g
Cholesterol	0 mg
Sodium	136 mg
Potassium	259 mg

In a medium saucepan cook carrots, covered, in a small amount of boiling, lightly salted water 4 to 6 minutes or till nearly tender. Drain; remove from pan. ▼ **For glaze,** in the same saucepan combine the green onion, honey, margarine or butter, and ginger. Cook and stir over medium heat till combined. Stir in the carrots. Cook, uncovered, about 2 minutes or till glazed, stirring frequently. Season to taste with pepper. *To roll-cut carrots, hold a knife or cleaver at a 45-degree angle to the cutting surface to make the first cut, then give food a quarter- to half-turn before angle-cutting again.

28

GREEN ONIONS

Creamed Chicken with Green Onion Biscuits

Makes 5 servings

Per Serving

Calories	447
Protein	26 g
Carbohydrate	26 g
Total Fat	26 g
Saturated Fat	8 g
Cholesterol	78 mg
Sodium	680 mg
Potassium	381 mg

1 cup all-purpose flour
1½ teaspoons baking powder
1½ teaspoons sugar
¼ teaspoon cream of tartar
⅛ teaspoon salt
¼ cup margarine or butter
⅓ cup half-and-half, light cream, *or* milk
2 green onions, thinly sliced (¼ cup)
1 clove garlic, minced
▼
1 cup sliced mushrooms
4 green onions, cut into ½-inch pieces(½ cup)

2 tablespoons margarine *or* butter
3 tablespoons all-purpose flour
1 cup chicken broth
½ cup half-and-half, light cream, or milk
½ cup shredded process Swiss cheese (2 ounces)
1 tablespoon dry white wine
2 cups cubed cooked chicken *or* turkey
Green onion slices or fans (optional)

Another time, try these savory biscuits spread with cream cheese.

In a medium mixing bowl stir together the 1 cup flour, baking powder, sugar, cream of tartar, and the ⅛ teaspoon salt. Cut in ¼ cup margarine or butter till mixture resembles coarse crumbs. Make a well in the center of the dry ingredients; add the ⅓ cup half-and-half, the ¼ cup green onion, and garlic all at once. Using a fork, stir *just till moistened.*
▼ **Turn dough** out on a lightly floured surface. Quickly knead dough for 10 to 12 strokes. Lightly roll or pat dough to ½-inch thickness. Cut with a floured 2½-inch biscuit cutter, dipping cutter into flour between cuts. Transfer biscuits to an ungreased baking sheet. Bake in a 450° oven for 10 to 12 minutes or till golden. ▼ **In a medium saucepan** cook the mushrooms and the ½ cup green onion in the 2 tablespoons margarine or butter till tender but not brown. Stir in the 3 tablespoons flour. Add chicken broth and the ½ cup half-and-half all at once. Cook and stir over medium heat till thickened and bubbly. Cook and stir for 1 minute more. Add cheese and wine, stirring till cheese melts. Stir in the cooked chicken or turkey; heat through. Serve over warm biscuits. Garnish each serving with green onion slices or fans, if desired.

Smoky New Potatoes And Peas

Makes 4 servings

Kids really go for the creamy cheese and bacon flavors in this side dish.

1 **pound whole tiny new potatoes, halved (about 12)**
1 **cup shelled peas**

▼

1 **tablespoon margarine** *or* **butter**
4 **teaspoons all-purpose flour**

1 **cup milk**
½ **of a 6-ounce link cheese food with hickory smoke flavor, cut up**
2 **ounces packaged cheese spread, cut up**
3 **slices bacon, crisp-cooked, drained and crumbled**

Per Serving

Calories	340
Protein	15 g
Carbohydrate	38 g
Total Fat	15g
Saturated Fat	7 g
Cholesterol	30 mg
Sodium	591 mg
Potassium	795 mg

In a medium saucepan cook potatoes, covered, in a small amount of boiling water for 12 minutes. Add peas. Cover and cook about 3 minutes more or till potatoes are just tender. Drain well. ▼ **In the same saucepan** melt margarine or butter. Stir in flour. Add milk all at once. Cook and stir till thickened and bubbly. Cook and stir for 1 minute more. Reduce heat; add cheeses. Cook and stir just till cheeses melt. Stir in cooked potatoes, peas, and *half* of the bacon; heat through. Transfer to a serving dish. Top with remaining bacon. Serve warm.

New Potatoes Gruyère

Makes 6 servings

Per Serving

Calories	205
Protein	7 g
Carbohydrate	36 g
Total Fat	4 g
Saturated Fat	2 g
Cholesterol	12 mg
Sodium	85 mg
Potassium	716 mg

2 **pounds whole tiny new potatoes (24 to 32)**
1 **small onion, sliced and separated into rings**
▼
1 **tablespoon all-purpose flour**
⅛ **teaspoon garlic powder**
⅛ **teaspoon ground white pepper**

½ **cup milk**
¼ **cup chicken broth**
½ **cup shredded Gruyère cheese (2 ounces)**
   Snipped parsley (optional)

Gruyère cheese has a mild, nutty flavor similar to Swiss cheese.

Halve any large potatoes. **With a vegetable peeler,** peel a strip around the center of each potato. In a large saucepan cook the potatoes and onion in a small amount of boiling, salted water for 12 to 15 minutes or till potatoes are just tender. Drain well. ▼ **Meanwhile,** for cheese sauce, in a small saucepan combine the flour, garlic powder, and pepper. Stir in the milk and the broth all at once. Cook and stir over medium heat till thickened and bubbly. Cook and stir for 1 minute more. Reduce heat to low. Add the cheese; cook and stir just till cheese melts. Add the cheese sauce to the potatoes; heat through. Transfer to a serving bowl. Sprinkle with the snipped parsley, if desired.

New Potato Salad With Pesto Mayonnaise

Makes 4 servings

By leaving the skins on the new potatoes, you retain lots of nutritional value and add a little color to your salad.

¾ **pound whole tiny new potatoes, quartered (about 9)**

½ **pound asparagus, cut into 1-inch pieces (1⅓ cups)**

1 **medium carrot, cut into julienne strips (½ cup)**
▼
⅓ **cup Pesto (see recipe, page 57)**

¼ **cup mayonnaise or salad dressing**

2 **green onions, thinly sliced (¼ cup)**

¼ **cup sliced pitted ripe olives**

¼ **teaspoon coarsely ground pepper**
▼
Milk (optional)

2 **tablespoons finely shredded Parmesan *or* Romano cheese**

Per Serving

Calories	364
Protein	9 g
Carbohydrate	31 g
Total Fat	25 g
Saturated Fat	4 g
Cholesterol	15 mg
Sodium	291 mg
Potassium	729 mg

Cook potatoes, covered, in a small amount of boiling, salted water for 8 minutes. Add the asparagus pieces and carrot; cook for 4 to 8 minutes more or till potatoes are just tender and asparagus and carrots are crisp-tender. Drain well. ▼ **In a large mixing bowl** stir together the Pesto and mayonnaise or salad dressing. Add the potatoes, asparagus, carrot strips, green onion, olives, and pepper. Stir till well combined. Cover and chill for 4 to 24 hours. ▼ **Just before serving,** stir in 1 or 2 tablespoons milk to moisten, if necessary. Sprinkle with Parmesan or Romano cheese.

New Potato And Avocado Salad

Makes 4 servings

Per Serving

Calories	327
Protein	4 g
Carbohydrate	30 g
Total Fat	23 g
Saturated Fat	4 g
Cholesterol	3 mg
Sodium	197 mg
Potassium	777 mg

1 pound whole tiny new potatoes, quartered (about 12)
▼
¼ cup red wine vinegar or vinegar
¼ cup olive oil or salad oil
1 to 2 tablespoons snipped fresh dill or 1 to 2 teaspoons dried dillweed
¼ teaspoon salt

⅛ teaspoon pepper
2 green onions, chopped (¼ cup)
▼
1 medium avocado, seeded, peeled, and cut into bite-size pieces
2 slices bacon, crisp-cooked, drained, and crumbled

Stir about 2 cups of cooked chicken or turkey, cut into bite-size strips, into this dill-flavored salad and you've got yourself a great-tasting luncheon or dinner entrée.

Cook potatoes, covered, in a small amount of boiling, salted water for 12 to 15 minutes or till just tender. Drain well. Transfer to a large salad bowl. Set aside. ▼ **For dressing,** in a screw-top jar combine red wine vinegar or vinegar, olive oil or salad oil, dill, salt, and pepper. Cover and shake well. Pour the dressing over the potatoes in the salad bowl. Toss gently to coat potatoes. Add green onion. Toss lightly to mix. Cover and chill for 4 to 24 hours. ▼ **To serve,** stir in avocado pieces. Sprinkle with crumbled bacon.

Basil Peas and Mushrooms

Makes 4 servings

Per Serving

Calories	101
Protein	5 g
Carbohydrate	15
Total Fat	3 g
Saturated Fat	1 g
Cholesterol	0 mg
Sodium	182 mg
Potassium	390 mg

2 cups shelled peas
1 medium carrot, sliced (½ cup)

▼

1 cup sliced mushrooms
1 cup sliced shiitake mushrooms
2 green onions, cut into ½-inch pieces (¼ cup)

1 tablespoon margarine *or* butter
1 tablespoon snipped fresh basil or ½ teaspoon dried basil, crushed
¼ teaspoon salt
Dash pepper

Shiitake (*shih TOCK ee*) mushrooms are a brown Oriental mushroom with a large, floppy cap, a tough, slender stem, and a rich, meaty flavor. If you have trouble locating them, substitute another mushroom.

Cook peas, covered, in a small amount of boiling salted water for 3 minutes. Add the carrots. Cook for 7 to 9 minutes more or till peas and carrots are crisp-tender. Drain well. Remove from the pan. ▼ **In the same saucepan** cook the mushrooms and onion in margarine or butter till onion is tender but not brown. Stir in the basil, salt, and pepper. Add the carrots and peas. Heat through. Serve immediately.

35

Peas with Fresh Mint And Cashews

Makes 4 servings

Refrigerate green peas in their pods, unwashed, in a plastic bag for up to 2 days. Shell just before using.

2 cups shelled peas
¼ cup chopped onion
▼
1 tablespoon margarine *or* butter
1 tablespoon snipped fresh mint *or* 1 teaspoon dried mint, crushed

⅛ teaspoon salt
¼ cup chopped dry-roasted cashews

Per Serving

Calories	135
Protein	5 g
Carbohydrate	14 g
Total Fat	7 g
Saturated Fat	1 g
Cholesterol	0 mg
Sodium	104 mg
Potassium	249 mg

Cook peas and onion, covered, in a small amount of boiling, salted water for 10 to 12 minutes or till crisp-tender. Drain well. ▼ **Stir in** margarine or butter, mint, and salt. Heat through. Sprinkle with cashews. Serve immediately.

SUGAR SNAP PEAS

Sugar Snap Peas With Orange Butter

Makes 4 servings

Per Serving

Calories	73
Protein	2 g
Carbohydrate	10 g
Total Fat	3 g
Saturated Fat	0 g
Cholesterol	0 mg
Sodium	125 mg
Potassium	218 mg

2 **medium carrots, cut into julienne strips (1 cup)**
½ **pound sugar snap peas (about 2 cups), tips and strings removed**
▼
½ **teaspoon finely shredded orange peel**

1 **tablespoon orange juice**
2 **teaspoons sugar**
⅛ **teaspoon salt**
⅛ **teaspoon ground ginger**
⅛ **teaspoons pepper**
1 **tablespoon margarine or butter**

Sugar snap peas (sometimes called sugar peas) are sweet, tender pods that have fully developed, plump, rounded peas inside. Refrigerate sugar snap peas in a plastic bag for up to 3 days.

Cook carrots, covered, in a small amount of boiling, salted water for 3 minutes. Add sugar snap peas and cook, covered, for 2 to 4 minutes more or till vegetables are crisp-tender. Drain well. ▼ **In a small mixing bowl** combine orange peel, orange juice, sugar, salt, ginger, and pepper. Pour over hot cooked carrots and peas; add margarine or butter. Toss lightly to coat.

SNOW PEAS

Snow Pea Salad with Sesame-Soy Vinaigrette

Makes 4 servings

Snow peas, also known as pea pods, are tender and sweet with a crisp, firm texture. The tiny peas inside are small and flat.

4 cups torn Chinese cabbage

1 cup snow peas, halved crosswise

½ cup mushrooms, quartered, or straw mushrooms, halved

1 medium carrot, thinly bias-sliced (½ cup)

1 green onion, thinly sliced (2 tablespoons)

▼

3 tablespoons vinegar

3 tablespoons salad oil

2 teaspoons soy sauce

1 teaspoon sugar

⅛ teaspoon toasted sesame oil

Dash cracked black pepper

2 teaspoons toasted sesame seeds

Per Serving

Calories	149
Protein	3 g
Carbohydrate	11 g
Total Fat	11 g
Saturated Fat	2 g
Cholesterol	0 mg
Sodium	200 mg
Potassium	350 mg

In a large mixing bowl combine cabbage, snow peas, mushrooms, carrot, and green onion. Toss lightly to mix. ▼ **For vinaigrette,** in a screw-top jar combine vinegar, salad oil, soy sauce, sugar, sesame oil, and pepper. Cover and shake well. Pour dressing over cabbage mixture. Add sesame seeds; toss lightly to mix.

FIDDLEHEAD FERNS

For a short time each spring, fiddleheads, which are the tightly curled, edible green shoots of any species of fern, make an appearance. Most commercially grown fiddlehead ferns are from the ostrich fern, and are 2 to 5 inches long and 1½ inches in diameter. Although their texture is similar to green beans, the flavor of these prized delicacies is like a cross between asparagus and green beans.

Look for fresh fiddlehead ferns at a farmer's market from April to June. Select those that are firm, tightly curled, and brightly colored. Refrigerate fiddlehead ferns, unwashed, in a plastic bag for up to 2 days. Wash them thoroughly before using.

You can eat fiddlehead ferns raw in salads, stir-fried with other vegetables, or steamed and served with butter.

Note: Fiddlehead ferns that are found in the wild should only be used if a knowledgeable person has determined that they are an edible variety.

Spring Fiddlehead Fern Salad

Makes 4 servings

Per Serving

Calories	141
Protein	3 g
Carbohydrate	7 g
Total Fat	13 g
Saturated Fat	1 g
Cholesterol	0 mg
Sodium	11 mg
Potassium	245 mg

16 fiddlehead ferns

▼

3 tablespoons almond oil
   or salad oil
3 tablespoons tarragon
   vinegar
1 teaspoon sugar

▼

Red-tipped leaf lettuce
1 cup small whole mush-
   rooms
2 tablespoons slivered
   almonds, toasted

Wash fiddlehead ferns thoroughly under running water; set aside. ▼ **For dressing,** in a screw-top jar combine almond oil or salad oil, vinegar, and sugar. Cover and shake well. ▼ **Line** 4 salad plates with lettuce leaves. Arrange fiddlehead ferns and mushrooms on lettuce. Shake dressing well; pour over each serving. Sprinkle almonds over each salad.

TOMATILLOS

*T*his small, olive green fruit, despite its name and appearance, is not related to the tomato. Its texture is like that of a firm tomato, though (with lots of seeds), and its flavor is rather acidic, with hints of lemon and apple. Fresh tomatillos, available year-round, are covered with a thin, papery, brown husk that is removed before using.

Select firm tomatillos with tight-fitting, dry husks. Avoid shriveled and bruised ones. Cover and refrigerate tomatillos for up to 10 days.

Tomatillos are most often used in Mexican and Tex-Mex salsas or salads.

Tomatillo Salsa
Makes about 1½ cups

½ **pound large tomatillos, husked and finely chopped (about 1 cup)**
1 **stalk celery, finely chopped (½ cup)**
1 **small onion, finely chopped (⅓ cup)**
2 **serrano* *or* jalapeño peppers, finely chopped**
2 **tablespoons snipped fresh cilantro *or* parsley**
2 **cloves garlic, minced**
¼ **teaspoons salt**

Per Serving	
Calories	5
Protein	0 g
Carbohydrate	1g
Total Fat	0g
Saturated Fat	0 g
Cholesterol	181 mg
Sodium	25mg
Potassium	43mg

In a medium mixing bowl stir together tomatillos, celery, onion, serrano or jalapeño peppers, cilantro or parsley, garlic, and salt. Cover and refrigerate for up to 2 days. Drain off excess liquid before serving.
*Serrano peppers are much hotter than jalapeño peppers, so adjust the amount you use according to your taste.

CABBAGE

Honey-Mustard Slaw

Makes 4 to 6 servings

Per Serving

Calories	215
Protein	3 g
Carbohydrate	24 g
Total Fat	14 g
Saturated Fat	2 g
Cholesterol	0 mg
Sodium	176 mg
Potassium	371 mg

3 cups shredded green
  cabbage (about ½ of a
  medium head)
2 medium carrots,
  shredded (1 cup)
1 medium pear *or* apple,
  cored and coarsely
  chopped (1 cup)

▼

3 tablespoons salad oil
3 tablespoons coarse-grain
  brown mustard *or*
  Dijon-style mustard
2 tablespoons lemon juice
2 tablespoons honey
1 clove garlic, minced
2 tablespoons chopped
  peanuts *or* cashews

Choose a red pear or apple to add color to this tasty side salad.

In a large mixing bowl stir together the cabbage, shredded carrot, and chopped pear or apple; set aside. ▼ **For dressing,** in a screw-top jar combine salad oil, mustard, lemon juice, honey, and garlic. Cover and shake well; pour over the cabbage mixture. Toss lightly to coat. Cover and chill for 2 to 24 hours. Sprinkle the slaw with peanuts or cashews before serving.

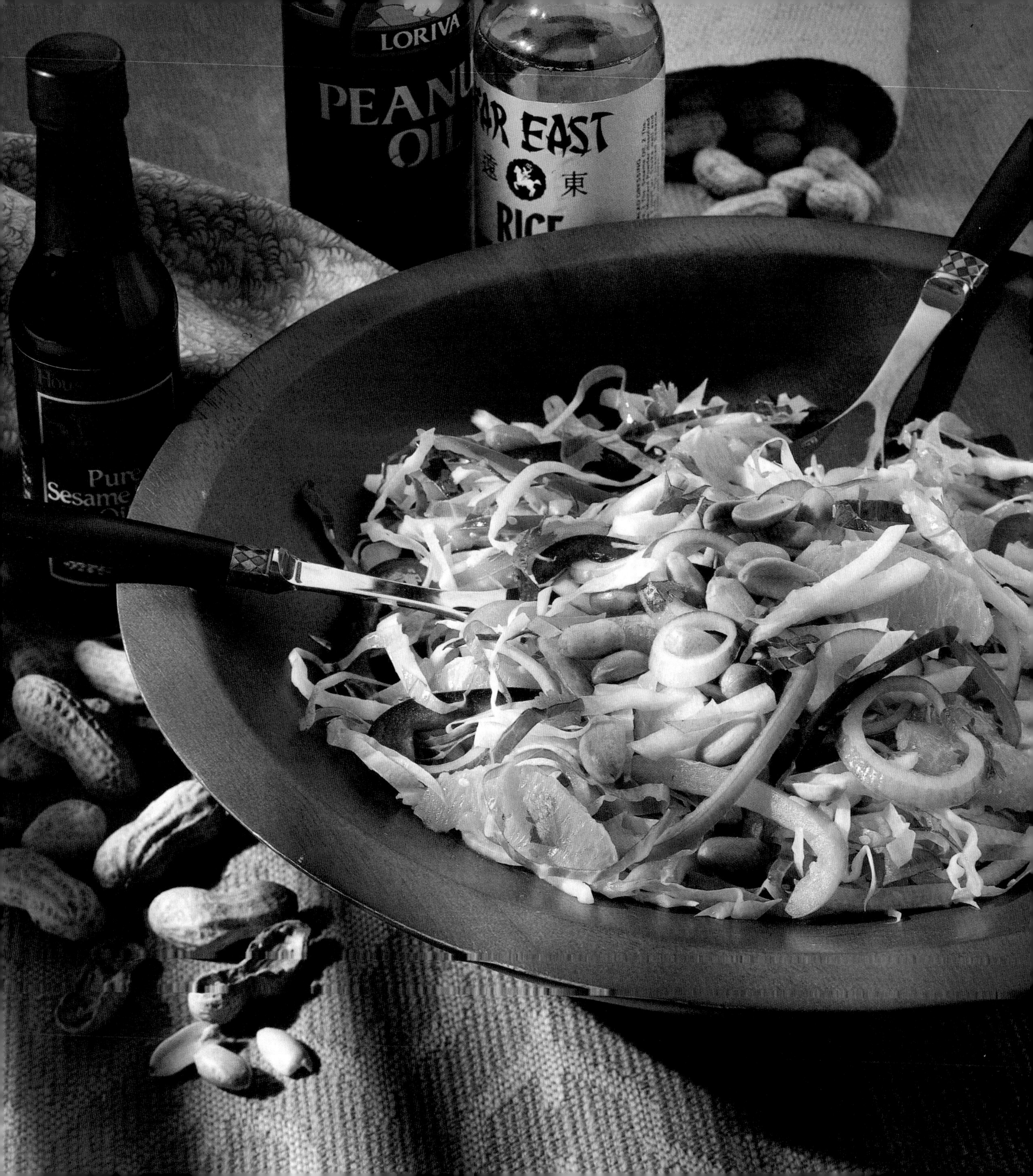

LORIVA
PEANU
OIL
AR EAST
遠
東
RICE
Pure
Sesame
Oil

Singapore Slaw

Makes 6 to 8 servings

Per Serving

Calories	125
Protein	3 g
Carbohydrate	12 g
Total Fat	8 g
Saturated Fat	1 g
Cholesterol	0 mg
Sodium	64 mg
Potassium	177 mg

3 cups shredded cabbage *or* ½ of a 16-ounce bag shredded cabbage with carrot

1½ cups jicama cut into strips

1 orange, peeled and sectioned

½ of a medium green, red, *or* yellow sweet pepper, cut into julienne strips (½ cup)

1 small red onion, thinly sliced and separated into rings

2 tablespoons snipped fresh cilantro
▼
2 tablespoons peanut oil *or* salad oil

4 teaspoons rice vinegar

1 tablespoon sugar

1 teaspoon toasted sesame seed (optional)

1 teaspoon toasted sesame oil

1 teaspoon soy sauce

¼ teaspoon dry mustard

¼ cup peanuts

Sweet peppers and oranges color this tangy slaw, which is tossed with a sesame dressing.

In a large mixing bowl combine cabbage, jicama, orange sections, sweet pepper, red onion, and cilantro. Cover and chill up to 4 hours.
▼ **For dressing,** in a screw-top jar combine peanut oil or salad oil, rice vinegar, sugar, sesame seed (if desired), toasted sesame oil, soy sauce, and dry mustard. Cover and shake well; pour over salad. Toss lightly to coat. Sprinkle with peanuts.

Greens with Blue Cheese And Snappy Nuts

Makes 4 servings

The hot and spicy nuts and the sharp, tangy blue cheese spark the flavor in this garden-fresh salad.

2 tablespoons walnut oil *or* salad oil

2 tablespoons white wine vinegar

⅛ teaspoon pepper

▼

3 cups torn Boston *or* Bibb lettuce

1 large apple or pear, cored and sliced (1¼ cups)

1 cup torn red-tipped leaf lettuce

¼ cup Snappy Nuts

¼ cup crumbled blue cheese (1 ounce)

Per Serving

Calories	437
Protein	9 g
Carbohydrate	18 g
Total Fat	40 g
Saturated Fat	5 g
Cholesterol	5 mg
Sodium	160 mg
Potassium	468 mg

For dressing, in a screw-top jar combine walnut oil or salad oil, white wine vinegar, and pepper. Cover and shake well. ▼ **In a large salad bowl** combine Boston or Bibb lettuce, sliced apple or pear, leaf lettuce, Snappy Nuts, and blue cheese. Shake dressing well; pour over salad. Toss lightly to coat.

Snappy Nuts

In a medium saucepan melt 1 tablespoon *margarine or butter.* Stir in 1 teaspoon *Worcestershire sauce,* ½ teaspoon *chili powder,* ½ teaspoon ground *red pepper,* and dash *garlic powder.* Add 1½ cups broken *walnuts or pecans,* stirring till nuts are evenly coated. Transfer nuts to a baking sheet. Bake in a 300° oven for 20 minutes, stirring twice. Let cool on sheet for 15 minutes. Turn out onto paper towels to finish cooling. Makes 1½ cups.

GREENS

Tossed Salad with Creamy Parmesan Dressing

Makes 4 servings

Per Serving

Calories	107
Protein	5 g
Carbohydrate	10 g
Total Fat	6 g
Saturated Fat	3 g
Cholesterol	14 mg
Sodium	121 mg
Potassium	391 mg

3 cups torn leaf lettuce
1 cup shredded red cabbage
1 medium yellow *or* red
    sweet pepper, cut into
    ¾ inch pieces (1 cup)
1 cup red and/or yellow
    baby pear tomatoes *or*
    cherry tomatoes, halved

▼
⅓ cup dairy sour cream
¼ cup very finely shredded
    Parmesan cheese
1 tablespoon red wine
    vinegar
1 teaspoon sugar
½ teaspoon Dijon-style
    mustard
1 to 2 tablespoons milk

Try tossing some seasoned croutons into this easy side salad.

In a large salad bowl combine leaf lettuce, red cabbage, sweet pepper, and tomato halves. ▼ **For dressing,** in a small mixing bowl stir together sour cream, Parmesan cheese, vinegar, sugar, and mustard. Pour dressing over salad. If necessary, stir in milk to make the dressing the desired consistency. Toss lightly to coat.

Beyond Lettuce

There are many salad greens available today. Here's a quick rundown on what you may find at your local farmer's market.
Butterhead: Small, loosely packed leaves; subtly sweet, buttery flavor. Boston and Bibb lettuce both are butterhead varieties. Red-tipped butterhead also is available.
Spinach: Crinkled or smooth-textured leaves with long stems; somewhat earthy flavor.

Romaine: Large, elongated, sturdy leaves that branch from a white base; slightly sharp flavor. Red-tipped romaine also is available.
Leaf lettuce: Sprawling, curly, crisp, yet tender leaves; sweet and delicate flavor. Red-tipped leaf lettuce also is available.
Radicchio: Ruby-red leaves with thick, white veins that form a small, round, compact head; bitter and peppery tasting.

Wilted Spinach And Muenster Salad

Makes 4 servings

A hot bacon and vinegar dressing warms the cheese just enough to soften it slightly—yum!

6 cups torn spinach *or* torn romaine
1 cup sliced mushrooms
1 small onion, chopped (⅓ cup)

▼

3 slices bacon
2 tablespoons vinegar *or* white wine vinegar
1 teaspoon sugar

½ teaspoon lemon-pepper seasoning
¼ teaspoon salt
4 ounces cubed Muenster *or* mozzarella cheese (1 cup)
1 medium tomato, cut into wedges
Coarsely cracked black pepper

Per Serving

Calories	227
Protein	11 g
Carbohydrate	8 g
Total Fat	18 g
Saturated Fat	9 g
Cholesterol	37 mg
Sodium	592 mg
Potassium	693 mg

In a large salad bowl combine spinach or romaine, mushrooms, and onion. Set aside. ▼ **In a 12-inch skillet** cook bacon over medium heat till crisp. Remove bacon, reserving drippings in skillet. Drain bacon on paper towels; crumble and set aside. Stir vinegar or white wine vinegar, sugar, lemon-pepper seasoning, and salt into reserved drippings; bring just to boiling. Remove from heat. Add the spinach mixture to skillet. Toss for 30 to 60 seconds or till spinach is just wilted. Add cheese and tomato wedges. Toss lightly to mix. Transfer to a serving bowl. Sprinkle with coarsely cracked black pepper. Serve immediately.

GREENS

Fresh Greens with Fontina

Makes 4 servings

Per Serving

Calories	276
Protein	10 g
Carbohydrate	8 g
Total Fat	23 g
Saturated Fat	7 g
Cholesterol	33 mg
Sodium	349 mg
Potassium	371 mg

4 cups torn spinach
½ cup watercress, stems
    removed
▼
2 tablespoons olive oil or
    salad oil
2 tablespoons dry red wine
1½ teaspoons lemon juice
1 teaspoon Dijon-style
    mustard
½ teaspoon sugar
    Freshly ground black
    pepper

▼
2 tablespoons olive oil *or*
    salad oil
¼ cup fine dry bread
    crumbs
1 teaspoon dried Italian
    seasoning, crushed
▼
4 ounces fontina cheese,
    cut into 8 wedges

Start an elegant dinner with this salad of mellow baked cheese, spinach, watercress, and a splash of red wine dressing.

In a large mixing bowl toss together spinach and watercress. Set aside. ▼ **For dressing,** in a screw-top jar combine 2 tablespoons olive oil or salad oil, dry red wine, lemon juice, mustard, sugar, and pepper. Cover and shake well. Set aside. ▼ **Pour** 2 tablespoons olive oil or salad oil into a small, shallow bowl. In another small, shallow bowl combine bread crumbs and Italian seasoning. ▼ **Dip each wedge** of fontina cheese in olive oil or salad oil, coating thoroughly. Roll each cheese wedge in the bread crumb mixture, covering all sides. Place cheese wedges on the unheated rack of a broiler pan. Don't let the sides of the cheese touch. Broil about 3 inches from the heat for 2 minutes or till brown and slightly softened. Watch cheese closely while broiling. Do not overcook or cheese will melt. ▼ **To serve,** shake dressing well; pour over greens. Toss lightly to coat. Divide greens among 4 salad plates. Place 2 warm cheese wedges atop greens on each plate. Serve immediately.

Tossed Green Salad with Raspberry Vinaigrette

Makes 4 servings

For your greens, choose from spinach, sorrel, red-tipped leaf lettuce, or Boston or Bibb lettuce.

4 cups torn mixed greens
1 cup enoki mushrooms
   (3 ounces)

▼

Raspberry Vinaigrette

½ cup cubed creamy
   Havarti, Brie, or smoked
   cheddar cheese
   (2 ounces)
¼ cup slivered almonds or
   pinenuts, toasted

In a large mixing bowl combine torn mixed greens and mushrooms. Toss lightly to mix. Divide salad among 4 salad plates. ▼ **Shake** Raspberry Vinaigrette well; drizzle a scant 2 tablespoons of the vinaigrette over each salad. Sprinkle each salad with cheese and nuts.

Raspberry Vinaigrette

In a screw-top jar combine 3 tablespoons *raspberry vinegar,* 3 tablespoons *salad oil,* 1 tablespoon snipped *parsley,* and 1 teaspoon *sugar.* Cover and shake well. Makes ½ cup.

Per Serving

Calories	197
Protein	6 g
Carbohydrate	6 g
Total Fat	18 g
Saturated Fat	4 g
Cholesterol	14 mg
Sodium	106 mg
Potassium	299 mg

Lemony Caesar Salad With Bagel Croutons

Makes 6 servings

Per Serving

Calories	241
Protein	7 g
Carbohydrate	14 g
Total Fat	18 g
Saturated Fat	3 g
Cholesterol	40 mg
Sodium	343 mg
Potassium	336 mg

1   **egg**
⅓   **cup chicken broth**
2   **anchovy fillets** *or* **1 teaspoon anchovy paste**
3   **tablespoons olive oil**
1   **teaspoon finely shredded lemon peel**
2   **tablespoons lemon juice**
1   **easpoon Dijon-style mustard**

¼   **teaspoon white wine Worcestershire sauce**
▼
1   **clove garlic, halved**
10   **cups torn romaine**
1   **cup Bagel Croutons**
¼   **cup grated Parmesan cheese**
  Whole black peppercorns

Our updated version of Caesar salad features a cooked egg dressing instead of the traditional uncooked dressing. Using uncooked eggs in recipes such as this may lead to bacterial contamination.

For dressing, in a blender container or food processor bowl combine egg, chicken broth, anchovy fillets or paste, olive oil, lemon peel, lemon juice, mustard, and Worcestershire sauce. Cover and blend or process till smooth. Transfer dressing to a small saucepan. Cook and stir dressing over low heat for 8 to 10 minutes or till thickened. *Do not boil.* Transfer to a bowl. Cover surface with plastic wrap; chill for 2 to 24 hours.

▼ **To serve,** rub the inside of a wooden salad bowl with the cut sides of the garlic clove; discard garlic clove. Add romaine, Bagel Croutons, and Parmesan cheese to salad bowl. Pour dressing over salad. Toss lightly to coat. Transfer to individual salad plates. Grind peppercorns over each serving.

Bagel Croutons

Split 2 *onion bagels.* With the cut side down, slice each bagel half into ¼-inch-thick half moons. In a large skillet combine 3 tablespoons *margarine or butter,* 1 tablespoon *olive oil,* and 2 small cloves *garlic,* minced. Cook and stir till margarine or butter melts. Remove from heat. Stir bagel half moons into margarine mixture. ▼ **Spread** half moons in a single layer in a shallow baking pan. Bake in a 300° oven for 10 minutes. Stir; bake 10 to 15 minutes more or till dry and crisp. Cool. Store in an airtight container for up to 1 week. Makes about 2 cups.

Greek Garden Salad

Makes 4 to 6 servings

If you're an anchovy fan, add 1 tablespoon anchovy paste to the Garlic Vinaigrette when you get ready to shake it up.

2 cups torn romaine *or* spinach
1 cup torn leaf lettuce *or* iceberg lettuce
1 cup torn radicchio *or* shredded red cabbage
▼
1 medium tomato
½ of a medium red onion

½ of a small cucumber
1 small green or red sweet pepper, cut into julienne strips (¾ cup)
¼ cup Greek olives or sliced pitted ripe olives
   Garlic Vinaigrette
½ cup crumbled feta cheese (2 ounces)

Per Serving

Calories	166
Protein	4 g
Carbohydrate	8 g
Total Fat	14 g
Saturated Fat	4 g
Cholesterol	12 mg
Sodium	244 mg
Potassium	308 mg

In a large salad bowl combine romaine or spinach, leaf lettuce or iceberg lettuce, and radicchio or red cabbage; set aside. ▼ **Cut the tomato** into thin wedges; cut each wedge in half. Slice the onion and cucumber; cut each slice in half. Add tomato, onion, cucumber, pepper strips, and olives to the greens. Shake Garlic Vinaigrette well; pour over salad. Toss lightly to coat. Sprinkle with feta cheese.

Garlic Vinaigrette

In a screw-top jar combine 3 tablespoons *olive oil or salad oil;* 3 tablespoons *white wine vinegar or vinegar;* 1 tablespoon snipped fresh *oregano or* 1 teaspoon dried *oregano,* crushed; 2 large cloves *garlic,* minced; and ⅛ teaspoon *pepper.* Cover and shake well. Makes about ½ cup dressing.

Summer Harvest Salad With Tarragon Dressing

Makes 4 servings

This is a great tossed salad to serve alongside grilled salmon fillets or tuna steaks.

¼ pound yellow wax beans *or* green beans, cut into 1-inch pieces (1 cup)

▼

3 tablespoons olive oil *or* salad oil
3 tablespoons white wine vinegar
1 tablespoon snipped fresh tarragon or ½ teaspoon dried tarragon, crushed

1 tablespoon water
1 tablespoon Dijon-style mustard
1 clove garlic, minced

▼

4 cups torn mixed greens
1 small zucchini *or* yellow summer squash, sliced (1 cup)
1 medium tomato, cut into wedges

Per Serving

Calories	80
Protein	2 g
Carbohydrate	7 g
Total Fat	6 g
Saturated Fat	1 g
Cholesterol	0 mg
Sodium	57 mg
Potassium	402 mg

Cook beans, covered, in a small amount of boiling salted water for 20 to 25 minutes or till tender. Drain. Cover and chill for at least 1 hour. ▼ **Meanwhile, for dressing,** in a screw-top jar combine olive oil or salad oil, white wine vinegar, tarragon, water, mustard, and garlic. Cover and shake well. ▼ **In a large salad bowl** combine mixed greens, zucchini slices, tomato wedges, and cooked beans. Shake dressing well; pour about *half* of the dressing over salad. Toss lightly to coat. Cover and store remaining dressing in the refrigerator for up to 2 weeks.

GREENS

Tossed Spinach Salad

Makes 4 servings

Per Serving

Calories	148
Protein	4 g
Carbohydrate	7 g
Total Fat	13 g
Saturated Fat	2 g
Cholesterol	0 mg
Sodium	82 mg
Potassium	489 mg

3 tablespoons salad oil

2 tablespoons water

2 tablespoons lemon juice

1 teaspoon sugar

1 teaspoon Dijon-style mustard

⅛ teaspoon pepper

1 clove garlic, minced

▼

4 cups torn spinach

1 cup shredded red cabbage

1 cup sliced cauliflower flowerets

2 green onions, thinly sliced (¼ cup)

2 tablespoons shelled sunflower seeds

Coarsely ground black pepper (optional)

If you're interested in experimenting with edible flowers, add a few to this salad. Try either nasturtiums or calendulas—both will add a slight peppery flavor.

For dressing, in a screw-top jar combine salad oil, water, lemon juice, sugar, mustard, pepper, and garlic. Cover and shake well. ▼ **In a large mixing bowl** combine spinach, cabbage, cauliflower, green onion, and sunflower seeds. Shake dressing well; pour over salad. Toss lightly to coat. If desired, sprinkle with pepper.

Stir-Fried Pork Salad With Peaches

Makes 4 main-dish servings

To toast ¼ cup or less of nuts, place the nuts in a small skillet. Cook and stir over medium heat for 5 to 7 minutes or till nuts are golden brown.

¾ **pound lean boneless pork**
2 **medium peaches, peeled, pitted, and sliced (2 cups)**
▼
1 **tablespoon lemon juice**
¾ **cup chicken broth**
¼ **cup maple syrup or maple-flavored syrup**
2 **tablespoons cornstarch**
2 **tablespoons snipped fresh chives**
2 **tablespoons peach brandy**
¼ **teaspoon salt**

¼ **teaspoon pepper**
▼
4 **cups torn Boston** *or* **Bibb lettuce**
2 **cups torn escarole** *or* **curly endive**
2 **cups torn radicchio** *or* **shredded red cabbage**
▼
1 **tablespoon cooking oil**
▼
¼ **cup sliced almonds, toasted**

Per Serving

Calories	323
Protein	16 g
Carbohydrate	33 g
Total Fat	13 g
Saturated Fat	3 g
Cholesterol	38 mg
Sodium	342 mg
Potassium	709 mg

Trim fat from the pork. Partially freeze the pork about 30 minutes. Thinly slice across the grain into bite-size pieces. Set pork aside. Toss peach slices with lemon juice to prevent darkening. Set aside. ▼ **For sauce,** in a small mixing bowl stir together the chicken broth, maple syrup, cornstarch, chives, peach brandy, salt, and pepper. Set aside. ▼ **In a large mixing bowl** combine Boston or Bibb lettuce, escarole or curly endive, and radicchio or shredded red cabbage. Toss lightly to mix. Divide the greens among 4 dinner plates. Arrange peach slices on greens. Set plates aside. ▼ **Pour cooking oil** into a wok or large skillet. (Add more oil as necessary during cooking.) Preheat wok over medium-high heat. Add pork to the wok and stir-fry 2 to 3 minutes or till no longer pink. Push the pork from the center of the wok. Stir the sauce; add to the center of the wok. Cook and stir till thickened and bubbly. Stir in pork to coat with sauce. Cook and stir about 1 minute more or till heated through. ▼ **Spoon the hot** pork mixture atop the greens and peaches on each dinner plate. Sprinkle with the slivered almonds.

Oriental Grilled Beef Salad

Makes 4 main-dish servings

Per Serving

Calories	496
Protein	24 g
Carbohydrate	12 g
Total Fat	41 g
Saturated Fat	8 g
Cholesterol	63 mg
Sodium	58 mg
Potassium	722 mg

½ **cup salad oil**
½ **cup rice wine vinegar or white wine vinegar**
2 **teaspoons toasted sesame oil**
1 **teaspoon sugar**
1 **teaspoon grated gingerroot**
¼ **teaspoon ground red pepper**
2 **cloves garlic, minced**
▼
¾ **pound boneless beef sirloin steak, cut 1 inch thick**

▼
3 **cups torn romaine *or* leaf lettuce**
3 **cups torn curly endive *or* escarole**
1 **large red *or* yellow sweet pepper, cut into julienne strips (1¼ cups)**
1 **cup red and/or yellow baby pear tomatoes or cherry tomatoes, halved**
1 **cup enoki mushrooms (3 ounces)**
¼ **cup chopped pistachio nuts**

Tearing rather than cutting salad greens avoids bruising and browning the leaves. It also exposes more of the insides of the leaves, so they absorb salad dressing better.

For dressing, in a screw-top jar combine salad oil, vinegar, sesame oil, sugar, grated gingerroot, red pepper, and garlic. Cover and shake well.
▼ **Place steak in a plastic bag** set in a shallow dish. Pour *⅓ cup* dressing into plastic bag. Close bag and turn to coat well. Marinate in the refrigerator for 6 to 24 hours, turning bag occasionally. Cover and refrigerate remaining dressing. ▼ **Remove steak from bag,** reserving marinade. Place steak on an uncovered grill directly over *medium-hot* coals for 6 minutes. Turn and grill to desired doneness, allowing 6 to 9 minutes more for medium. Brush occasionally with reserved marinade.
▼ **For salad,** in a very large bowl combine romaine or leaf lettuce, curly endive or escarole, sweet pepper strips, tomatoes, and enoki mushrooms. Toss lightly to mix. Divide salad mixture among 4 plates. Thinly slice grilled steak and divide into 4 equal portions. Top each salad with meat. Sprinkle with pistachio nuts. Drizzle the reserved dressing over salads.

Chicken Salad with Blue Cheese Dressing

Makes 4 main-dish servings

Mesclun is a mixture of spicy and delicate baby lettuces grown in rows next to each other and harvested at the same time. The mixture is always a combination of flavors, textures, and colors.

8 cups mesclun *or* 6 cups
   torn romaine and 2 cups
   torn escarole *or* curly
   endive

1½ cups chopped cooked
   chicken *or* turkey (about
   8 ounces)

2 medium tomatoes, cut
   into wedges

1 cup jicama cut into
   juliene strips (about
   4 ounces)

1 medium yellow *or* green
   sweet pepper, cut into
   1-inch squares (1 cup)

½ cup garlic croutons

▼

½ cup Blue Cheese Dressing

Per Serving

Calories	220
Protein	22 g
Carbohydrate	13 g
Total Fat	9 g
Saturated Fat	4 g
Cholesterol	61 mg
Sodium	230 mg
Potassium	674 mg

In a large salad bowl combine mesclun, chicken, tomato wedges, jicama, yellow or green sweet pepper, and croutons. ▼ **Pour** Blue Cheese Dressing over salad. Toss lightly to coat.

Blue Cheese Dressing

In a blender container or food processor bowl combine ½ cup dairy *sour cream*; ¼ cup cream-style *cottage cheese*; ¼ cup crumbled *blue cheese*; 1 *green onion*, thinly sliced (2 tablespoons); ½ teaspoon finely shredded *lemon peel*; 1 teaspoon *lemon juice*; and ⅛ teaspoon *salt*. Cover and blend or process till smooth. Stir in enough *milk* (1 to 2 tablespoons) to make of desired consistency. Cover and store in the refrigerator for up to 2 weeks. Makes about 1 cup.

HERBS & FLOWERS

If you've been cooking with dried herbs, get ready for the surprising taste difference when you use fresh herbs from a farmer's market! And have you been longing to toss some of those colorful edible flowers into a salad? Read on and learn all about buying and using herbs and flowers in your cooking.

When purchasing fresh herbs, choose those with fresh-looking leaves that have no brown spots. Immerse the cut stems in water about 2 inches deep, cover the leaves loosely, and refrigerate for several days (a plastic bag makes a good covering). Remember, fresh herbs are highly perishable, so purchase them only as you need them.

When you're substituting fresh herbs for dried, start by tripling the amount of dried leaf herb called for in the recipe. For example, if a recipe uses 1 teaspoon of the dried herb, add 1 tablespoon of the fresh.

Like herbs, every variety of edible flower imparts a different flavor to food. The more fragrant a flower, the more flavor it imparts. Flowers may be used as an ingredient in foods or as a colorful garnish.

Choose flowers that are fresh and free of bruises. Before using, rinse flowers and gently pat dry. Store edible flowers in an airtight container in the refrigerator for up to 1 day.

Pesto

Makes ¾ cup

Per Serving

Calories	117
Protein	3 g
Carbohydrate	1 g
Total Fat	12 g
Saturated Fat	2 g
Cholesterol	3 mg
Sodium	79 mg
Potassium	56 mg

1 cup firmly packed fresh
  basil leaves
½ cup firmly packed
  parsley sprigs with
  stems removed
½ cup grated Parmesan or
  Romano cheese

¼ cup olive oil or cooking
  oil
¼ cup pine nuts or walnuts
1 large clove garlic, sliced
▼
¼ cup olive oil or cooking
  oil

For pesto, in a blender container or food processor bowl combine basil leaves, parsley, Parmesan or Romano cheese, nuts, garlic, and ¼ teaspoon *salt*. Cover and blend or process with several on-off turns till a paste forms, stopping the machine several times and scraping the sides.

▼ **With the machine** running slowly, gradually add oil and blend or process to the consistency of soft butter. Divide into 3 portions (about ¼ cup each) and place in small airtight containers. Refrigerate for 1 or 2 days or freeze for up to 1 month.

Edible Flowers & Herbs

Chives (with flowers) (Allium schoenoprasum)
Globe-shaped lavender flowers with a mild onion flavor; grasslike, round, hollow leaves with a mild onion flavor.

Nasturtiums (Tropaeolum majus)
Yellow, red, and orange flowers with a peppery, radishlike flavor; edible leaves.

Pansies (Viola x wittrockiana)
Soft, velvety flowers in many colors with a slightly spicy flavor.

Violets and Violas (Viola species)
Small, bluish purple flowers with a sweet, spicy, sometimes tangy flavor; edible leaves and stems.

Rose petals (Rosa species)
Red, pink, white, and yellow flowers with a velvety texture and a delicate, sweet flavor.

Calendulas (Calendula officinalis)
Yellow or gold flowers with a mild peppery taste.

Marigolds (Tagetes species)
Yellow and orange flowers with a mild peppery taste; *do not eat* leaves or stems.

Borage (Borago officinalis)
Purple and pink flowers with a sweet, cucumberlike flavor; edible, fuzzy, gray-green leaves that also taste like a cucumber.

Dianthus (Dianthus species)
Flat red, pink, or white flowers, some in two colors with a spicy, clovelike flavor and aroma.

Daylilies (Hemerocallis hybrids)
Flowers in many shades of orange and yellow with a slightly sweet, nutlike flavor.

Geraniums (Pelargonium species)
Pink, red, white, or purple flowers. Some varieties have flavored leaves, such as rose, lemon, mint, apple, and nutmeg.

Tarragon
Slender, dark green leaves; spicy, sharp flavor with licoricelike overtones.

Mint
Many varieties, each with different leaves. Spearmint, with light green, serrated, oval leaves, and peppermint with darker, smoother leaves are the most popular. All varieties taste sweet, cool, and refreshing. Recipes in this book were tested with spearmint, but any variety will taste delicious.

Choose Edible Flowers with Care
The best edible flowers are unsprayed blossoms from your own garden. Edible flowers also can be obtained from farmer's markets, the produce section of some supermarkets, local herb gardens, some restaurant or produce suppliers, and mail-order outlets.

Not all flowers and not all parts of all flowering plants are edible. Choose only those specified on page 58 or ones you know to be safe. Use flowers that have been grown without the use of pesticides or other chemicals. Do not use flowers from florist shops—they're usually treated with chemicals.

Summer savory
Small, narrow, pointed leaves; warm, peppery flavor and grassy fragrance.

Oregano
Small, pointed leaves; strong, spicy flavor with bitter undertones.

Cilantro
Flat, serrated leaves; pungent, almost musty fragrance and taste.

Dill
Tiny, feathery, bright green leaves; delicate, refreshing taste.

Thyme
Small, oval, grayish green leaves; heavy, spicy aroma with a pungent, clovelike taste.

Basil
Wide, oval, silky leaves with creases; flavor ranges from peppery and robust to sweet and spicy.

Italian parsley
Large, flat, dark green leaves; celerylike flavor.

Rosemary
Leathery, spiky leaves; pungent, piny flavor wth a sweet scent.

PEAK SEASON
GARLIC

Garlic is a strongly scented, pungent bulb of a plant that is related to the onion. Each bulb, or head, has a papery outer skin and is made up of several small segments called cloves. Each clove also has a papery skin.

Choose fresh garlic that's plump and feels firm.

Store the garlic in a cool, dry, dark place. Leave the bulbs whole because the individual cloves dry out quickly.

Most garlic is used as a seasoning but when whole heads are baked or roasted in the oven, the garlic becomes sweet and very mild.

Roasted Garlic Appetizer

Makes 4 appetizer servings

- 4 **whole heads garlic**
- 2 **tablespoons olive oil**
- 2 **tablespoons snipped fresh thyme** *or* **1 teaspoon dried thyme, crushed**
- ½ **teaspoon cracked black pepper**
- ¾ **cup chicken broth**

- ¼ **cup finely snipped dried tomatoes**

▼

- 4 **ounces chèvre cheese (goat cheese), sliced Fresh thyme**

▼

Italian bread

Per Serving

Calories	380
Protein	15 g
Carbohydrate	51 g
Total Fat	13 g
Saturated Fat	5 g
Cholesterol	13 mg
Sodium	574 mg
Potassium	359 mg

Peel the paperlike outer skin off the garlic heads. *Do not separate or peel individual cloves.* Arrange the garlic heads in a 8x8½-inch baking pan. Drizzle oil over garlic heads. Sprinkle with thyme and pepper. Pour chicken broth into pan. Sprinkle dried tomatoes around garlic heads. ▼ **Bake,** covered, in a 350° oven for 1 hour and 15 minutes or till garlic and tomatoes are tender, basting with chicken broth occasionally. Uncover and add chèvre cheese to dish. Bake, uncovered, about 10 minutes more or till cheese just begins to soften. Transfer to 4 individual serving bowls. Garnish with fresh thyme. ▼ **To serve,** slip the skins off the roasted cloves and spread onto Italian bread slices along with the melted chèvre cheese and dried tomatoes.

GREEN BEANS

Italian Green Beans With Bacon

Makes 4 to 5 servings

Per Serving

Calories	166
Protein	4 g
Carbohydrate	11 g
Total Fat	13 g
Saturated Fat	4 g
Cholesterol	11 mg
Sodium	160 mg
Potassium	364 mg

4 **slices bacon**

▼

¾ **pound Italian green beans, cut into 1-inch pieces (2¼ cups)**

▼

2 **medium carrots, thinly sliced (1 cup)**

1 **tablespoon margarine *or* butter**

1 **clove garlic, minced**

⅛ **to ¼ teaspoon pepper**

If Italian green beans, which have a wide, flat, green pod, aren't available, substitute the more slender and rounded regular green beans or the very skinny haricot verts.

In a large skillet cook the bacon over medium heat till crisp, turning occasionally. Remove bacon, reserving 2 tablespoons drippings in skillet. Drain bacon on paper towels. ▼ **Meanwhile, precook** green beans in a small amount of boiling salted water for 4 minutes; drain. ▼ **Add the partially cooked** green beans, carrots, margarine or butter, and garlic to reserved bacon drippings in skillet. Cook and stir over medium-high heat about 5 minutes or till vegetables are crisp-tender. Crumble bacon; stir bacon and pepper into vegetable mixture. Remove from heat. Transfer to a serving bowl.

GREEN BEANS

Green Bean Bundles In Sweet Pepper Sauce

Makes 4 servings

Per Serving

Calories	210
Protein	4 g
Carbohydrate	28 g
Total Fat	8 g
Saturated Fat	1 g
Cholesterol	0 mg
Sodium	292 mg
Potassium	685 mg

3 medium leeks (12 ounces)
▼
40 green beans (about ¾ pound)
▼
2 tablespoons olive oil *or* cooking oil
¾ cup dry white wine

2 tablespoons snipped fresh basil *or* oregano
½ teaspoon salt
▼
4 large red sweet peppers, chopped (4 cups)
2 large yellow sweet peppers, chopped (2 cups)

Rinse leeks several times with cold water. Remove any tough outer leaves. Trim roots from base. Separate 1 leaf (about 2 inches wide) from remaining leaves. In a skillet cook leaf, uncovered, in boiling water about 1 minute or till tender and bright green. Remove leaf; drain on paper towels. When cool, cut leaf lengthwise into eight ¼-inch-wide strips. ▼ **For bean bundles,** trim ends from beans. Gather beans into bunches of 5. Carefully tie each bundle with a cooled leek leaf strip. If necessary, trim ends of leek strip. Place a steamer basket in a saucepan. Add water to just below the bottom of steamer basket. Bring to boiling. Add bean bundles to basket. Cover and reduce heat. Steam for 18 to 22 minutes or till beans are tender. Season with salt and pepper. ▼ **Meanwhile,** for sauce, chop white part of leeks (about 1 cup). In the same large skillet cook chopped leek in 1 tablespoon of the hot oil about 5 minutes or till tender. Add the white wine, snipped basil or oregano, and salt. Reduce heat; cook about 3 minutes or till most of the liquid has evaporated. Set aside. ▼ **In another skillet,** cook chopped red pepper in the remaining oil about 10 minutes or till tender. Remove red pepper, reserving oil in skillet. In reserved oil cook chopped yellow pepper about 6 minutes or till tender. ▼ **In a blender** container or food processor bowl combine cooked red pepper and ⅔ *cup* of the sauce mixture. Cover and blend or process till smooth; set aside. In a clean blender container or food processor bowl combine cooked yellow pepper and remaining sauce mixture. Cover and blend or process till smooth. Serve sauces warm or at room temperature with bean bundles. Garnish with additional basil or oregano, if desired.

Green beans are often called string beans because at one time, the pods had tough strings along their sides that had to be removed before cooking. Today, the strings have been eliminated from all varieties of green beans.

GREEN BEANS

Summer Herbed Beans

Makes 4 servings

As an option to the tomato wedges, use a cup of bite-size red or yellow baby pear tomatoes in this colorful basil- and dill-flavored sauté.

½ **pound yellow wax beans, cut into 1-inch pieces (1½ cups)**
¼ **pound green beans, cut into 1-inch pieces (¾ cup)**
▼
2 **tablespoons snipped fresh basil *or* 2 teaspoons dried basil, crushed**
1 **tablespoon snipped fresh dill *or* 1 teaspoon dried dillweed**

1 **tablespoon melted margarine *or* butter**
¼ **teaspoon pepper Dash salt**
▼
1 **tablespoon olive oil *or* cooking oil**
1 **large tomato, cut into wedges**
½ **cup crumbled feta cheese (2 ounces)**

Per Serving

Calories	129
Protein	4 g
Carbohydrate	9 g
Total Fat	10 g
Saturated Fat	3 g
Cholesterol	12 mg
Sodium	32 mg
Potassium	346 mg

Precook wax beans and green beans, covered, in a small amount of boiling salted water for 4 minutes; drain well. ▼ **Meanwhile, for sauce,** in a small mixing bowl combine basil, dill, melted margarine or butter, pepper, and salt. Set sauce aside. ▼ **Pour the olive oil** or cooking oil into a wok or large skillet. (Add more oil as necessary during cooking.) Preheat over medium-high heat. Add the partially cooked beans to the wok or skillet; stir-fry about 3 minutes or till beans are crisp-tender. Add tomato wedges, feta cheese, and sauce to wok or skillet. Stir all ingredients together to coat with sauce. Heat through. Serve immediately.

GREEN BEANS

French-Style Green Beans With Lemon and Walnuts

Makes 4 servings

Per Serving

Calories	104
Protein	3 g
Carbohydrate	8 g
Total Fat	8 g
Saturated Fat	1 g
Cholesterol	0 mg
Sodium	37 mg
Potassium	297 mg

¾ **pound green beans, sliced lengthwise**

▼

¼ **cup chopped walnuts**
1 **teaspoon grated fresh gingerroot**

1 **tablespoon margarine *or* butter**
¼ **teaspoon finely shredded lemon peel**
1 **teaspoon lemon juice**

Fresh beans should be washed before you store them. Refrigerate them in airtight plastic bags for 3 to 4 days.

Cook beans, covered, in a small amount of boiling salted water for 10 to 15 minutes or till crisp-tender; drain. ▼ **Meanwhile, cook** and stir walnuts and gingerroot in margarine or butter over medium heat for 2 to 3 minutes or till nuts are toasted. Remove from heat and stir in lemon peel and lemon juice. Stir nut mixture into cooked beans.

TOMATOES

Three-Tomato Tart
Makes 10 to 12 appetizer servings

Per Serving

Calories	179
Protein	6 g
Carbohydrate	14 g
Total Fat	11 g
Saturated Fat	3 g
Cholesterol	9 mg
Sodium	134 mg
Potassium	135 mg

Pastry for Single-Crust Pie (see recipe, page 163)
3 tablespoons grated Parmesan cheese

▼
2 egg whites
1 cup low-fat ricotta cheese
2 cloves garlic, minced
1 tablespoon snipped fresh lemon thyme *or* thyme, *or* 1 teaspoon dried thyme, crushed

▼
2 large tomatoes, sliced
5 yellow *or* red cherry tomatoes, sliced
2 red cherry tomatoes, sliced
1 tablespoon olive oil *or* cooking oil
2 teaspoons snipped fresh lemon thyme *or* thyme, *or* ½ teaspoon dried thyme, crushed

Garnish this beautiful, carefree appetizer tart with sprigs of fresh tyme.

Prepare Pastry For Single-Crust Pie. On a lightly floured surface, roll pastry into a circle about 12 inches in diameter. Transfer to a 10-inch tart pan; ease pastry into pan. Trim pastry even with rim of pan. *Do not prick pastry.* Line pastry shell with a double thickness of foil. Bake pastry in a 450° oven for 5 minutes. Remove foil. Bake for 5 to 7 minutes more or till pastry is nearly done. Remove from oven. Reduce oven temperature to 325°. Sprinkle tart shell with Parmesan cheese.
▼ **Meanwhile, in a small mixing bowl** beat egg whites slightly. Stir in ricotta cheese, garlic, and the 1 tablespoon thyme; spread over pastry. ▼ **Overlap** large tomato slices in a circle around edge. Arrange yellow cherry tomato slices in a circle within the tomato ring. Fill center with red cherry tomato slices. Stir together olive oil or cooking oil and the 2 teaspoons thyme. Brush tomatoes with oil mixture.
▼ **Bake tart** in a 325° oven for 25 to 30 minutes or till heated through and nearly set. Serve warm or at room temperature. Refrigerate any leftover tart.

TOMATOES

Couscous-Stuffed Tomato Tulips

Makes 4 servings

½   cup water
¼   cup couscous
▼
2   tablespoons olive oil *or* salad oil
1   tablespoon finely chopped shallots *or* onion
1   tablespoon lemon juice
1   teaspoon Dijon-style mustard

⅛   teaspoon salt
⅛   teaspoon pepper
▼
¼   cup chopped peeled kohlrabi or jicama
¼   cup chopped yellow or green sweet pepper
▼
4   medium tomatoes
    Leaf lettuce (optional)

Per Serving

Calories	137
Protein	3 g
Carbohydrate	16 g
Total Fat	7 g
Saturated Fat	1 g
Cholesterol	0 mg
Sodium	113 mg
Potassium	349 mg

In a small saucepan bring water to boiling. Stir in couscous. Cover and let stand about 5 minutes or till liquid is absorbed. ▼ **Meanwhile, for marinade,** in a screw-top jar combine olive oil or salad oil, chopped shallots or onion, lemon juice, mustard, salt, and pepper. Cover and shake well. ▼ **In a small mixing bowl** combine couscous, kohlrabi or jicama, and yellow or green sweet pepper. Shake marinade; pour over couscous mixture. Cover and refrigerate for 2 to 24 hours. ▼ **To serve,** cut out ½ inch of the core from each tomato at the stem end. Invert tomatoes. Cutting from the top to, *but not through,* the stem end, cut each tomato into 6 wedges. Place tomatoes on lettuce-lined plates, if desired. Spread tomato wedges apart slightly; fill with the couscous mixture.

TOMATOES

Tomato-Sage Pasta

Makes 4 servings

Per Serving

Calories	185
Protein	5 g
Carbohydrate	32 g
Total Fat	4 g
Saturated Fat	1 g
Cholesterol	0 mg
Sodium	283 mg
Potassium	436 mg

2 **cloves garlic, minced**

1 **tablespoon olive oil** *or* **cooking oil**

1½ **pounds plum tomatoes, peeled and quartered**

¼ **teaspoon salt**

¼ **teaspoon pepper**

1 **small green or yellow sweet pepper, cut into julienne strips (½ cup)**

1 **tablespoon snipped fresh sage** *or* **1 teaspoon dried sage, crushed**

▼

4 **ounces packaged linguine or fettuccine**

Instead of linguine or fettuccine, toss this quick and easy sauce with penne or mostaccioli pasta—their tube shapes fill up with sauce.

For sauce, in a medium saucepan cook the garlic in hot oil for 30 seconds. Stir in the tomatoes, salt, and pepper. Bring to boiling; reduce heat. Simmer, uncovered, for 12 minutes. Stir in green or yellow sweet pepper and sage; cook about 5 minutes more or to desired consistency. ▼ **Meanwhile, cook pasta** according to package directions. Drain well. Toss pasta with sauce. Serve immediately.

Peeling Tomatoes

Ever struggle with peeling a tomato? Here's a trick to make it easier. Spear the tomato in the stem end with a fork, or hold in a slotted spoon, and plunge the tomato into boiling water for 30 seconds or just till the skin splits. Immediately dip the tomato into cold water. Using a sharp paring knife, pull the skin off the tomato. (HINT: Peel apricots and peaches the same way.)

TOMATOES

Freezer Tomato Sauce

Makes 3 or 4 pints

Plum tomatoes, sometimes called Italian or Roma tomatoes, are a thick and meaty, oval-shaped tomato. They have small seeds, little juice, and a mild, rich flavor. They're especially good for using in sauces.

6 **pounds plum tomatoes**
▼
3 **medium onions, chopped (1½ cups)**
1 **stalk celery, chopped (½ cup)**
3 **large cloves garlic, minced**
2 **tablespoons olive oil** *or* **cooking oil**
2 **teaspoons sugar**
1 **to 2 teaspoons salt**
½ **teaspoon pepper**

1 **fresh red cayenne chili pepper, seeded and finely chopped (½ teaspoon) or ⅛ teaspoon ground red pepper (optional)**
2 **tablespoons snipped fresh oregano** *or* **2 teaspoons dried oregano, crushed**
1 **to 2 tablespoons snipped fresh thyme** *or* **1 to 2 teaspoons dried thyme, crushed**

Per Serving

Calories	97
Protein	3 g
Carbohydrate	17 g
Total Fat	3 g
Saturated Fat	0 g
Cholesterol	0 mg
Sodium	206 mg
Potassium	675 mg

In a large kettle bring 4 inches of *water* to boiling. Immerse tomatoes in boiling water for 1 minute. Drain in a colander; peel, seed, and chop tomatoes. (You should have 10 cups.) ▼ **In the same kettle** cook onion, celery, and garlic in hot oil about 5 minutes or till tender. Add chopped tomatoes, sugar, salt, pepper, and cayenne pepper, if desired. Bring to boiling; reduce heat. Simmer, uncovered, for 45 minutes, stirring occasionally. Stir in oregano and thyme. Simmer, uncovered, for 15 minutes more. Cool slightly. ▼ **In a food processor bowl** process sauce, one fourth at a time, to desired texture. (Or, put sauce through a food mill.) Place sauce in a bowl set in ice water to cool quickly. Fill 3 or 4 freezer containers; seal tightly, label, and freeze. ▼ **To thaw one portion,** remove from freezer container and place in a saucepan. Cook over medium heat till hot, stirring occasionally. (Or, in a 1-quart microwave-safe casserole cook on 100% power (high) for 12 to 14 minutes, stirring occasionally.) Serve hot sauce over pasta.

TOMATOES

Tomato-Pesto Toast

Makes 12 to 16 slices

A great appetizer for your next summer cookout.

2 French-style rolls (about 6 inches long), bias sliced ½-inch thick

▼

Pesto (see recipe, page 57)

2 to 3 plum tomatoes, cut lengthwise into thin slices

⅓ cup crumbled feta cheese
Coarsely cracked black pepper

Per Serving

Calories	150
Protein	5 g
Carbohydrate	13 g
Total Fat	9 g
Saturated Fat	2 g
Cholesterol	6 mg
Sodium	233 mg
Potassium	118 mg

Arrange bread slices on the rack of an unheated broiler pan. Broil 4 to 5 inches from the heat about 1 minute on each side or till toasted.

▼ **Spread** a scant *1 tablespoon* Pesto on each slice of toasted bread; top each with a tomato slice. Crumble some of the feta cheese atop each tomato slice. Sprinkle with pepper. Watching carefully, broil 4 to 5 inches from the heat for 1 to 2 minutes or till heated through.

Corn and Barley Salad With Cilantro Dressing

Makes 4 to 6 servings

Per Serving

Calories	327
Protein	5 g
Carbohydrate	38 g
Total Fat	19 g
Saturated Fat	3 g
Cholesterol	0 mg
Sodium	212 mg
Potassium	333 mg

⅔ **cup water**
½ **cup quick-cooking barley**
▼
3 **medium ears of fresh corn**
▼
1 **small green sweet pepper, chopped (½ cup)**

1 **small red sweet pepper, chopped (½ cup)**
2 **green onions, thinly sliced (¼ cup)**
Cilantro Dressing
▼
Lettuce leaves
Fresh cilantro (optional)

Seed the jalapeño pepper before adding it to the Cilantro Dressing if you want a little less "zing" in your salad.

In a saucepan combine water and barley. Bring to boiling. Cover and reduce heat. Simmer for 10 to 12 minutes or till liquid is absorbed. ▼ **Meanwhile, remove the husks** from corn; scrub with a stiff brush to remove silks. Rinse. Use a sharp knife to remove corn from cobs, cutting two-thirds of the way to the cob. (You should have about 1½ cups.) Cook corn, covered, in a small amount of boiling unsalted water for 2 minutes; drain well. ▼ **In a large mixing bowl** combine cooked barley, corn, chopped green and red sweet pepper, and green onion. Pour Cilantro Dressing over barley mixture. Toss lightly to coat. Cover and chill for 4 to 24 hours. ▼ **To serve,** line a salad bowl with lettuce leaves. Transfer barley mixture to the lettuce-lined salad bowl. Garnish with fresh cilantro, if desired.

Cilantro Dressing

In a screw-top jar combine ⅓ cup *olive oil or salad oil;* ¼ cup snipped fresh *cilantro;* ¼ cup finely chopped *onion;* ¼ cup *lime juice;* 1 fresh *or* canned *jalapeño pepper,* finely chopped (2 tablespoons); 1 tablespoon *water;* ¼ teaspoon *salt;* and 1 clove *garlic,* minced. Cover and shake well. Makes about ¾ cup.

CORN

Corn Chowder

Makes 4 to 6 servings

Use fresh corn on the cob as soon as possible (purists say to put the pot of water on to boil before you even pick the corn). But, if you're forced to store it, refrigerate the corn for no more than 2 days.

4 medium ears of fresh corn
  ▼
1 cup water
½ cup cubed, peeled potato
1 medium onion, chopped (½ cup)
1 stalk celery, chopped (½ cup)
4 teaspoons instant chicken bouillon granules
¼ teaspoon pepper
1¾ cups milk

`1 tablespoon margarine or butter
2 tablespoons all-purpose flour
  ▼
4 slices bacon, crisp-cooked, drained, and crumbled
1 to 2 tablespoons snipped fresh cilantro or parsley
Salt
Cracked black pepper

Per Serving

Calories	256
Protein	10 g
Carbohydrate	37 g
Total Fat	9 g
Saturated Fat	3 g
Cholesterol	13 mg
Sodium	1082 mg
Potassium	595 mg

Remove the husks from corn; scrub with a stiff brush to remove silks. Rinse. Use a sharp knife to cut off just the kernel tips from the ears of corn, then scrape the cobs with the dull edge of the knife. (You should have about 2 cups.) ▼ **In a large saucepan** combine corn, water, potato, onion, celery, bouillon granules, and the ¼ teaspoon pepper. Bring to boiling. Cover and reduce heat. Simmer about 10 minutes or till corn and potatoes are just tender, stirring occasionally. Stir in *1½ cups* of the milk and the margarine or butter. Combine the remaining ¼ cup milk and the flour; stir into the corn mixture. Cook and stir till thickened and bubbly. Cook and stir for 1 minute more. ▼ **Ladle chowder** into soup bowls. Sprinkle with crumbled bacon and cilantro *or* parsley. Season to taste with salt and pepper.

Pickled Baby Corn on the Cob

Makes 8 to 10 servings

Per Serving

Calories	88
Protein	2 g
Carbohydrate	22 g
Total Fat	0 g
Saturated Fat	0 g
Cholesterol	0 mg
Sodium	8 mg
Potassium	311 mg

Baby corn is a miniature version that can be enjoyed cob and all.

1½ **cups sugar**
1 **cup vinegar**
½ **teaspoon ground turmeric**
½ **teaspoon celery seed**
¼ **teaspoon dry mustard**
1 **clove garlic, minced**
1½ **pounds fresh baby corn on the cob, husked**

In a large saucepan stir together sugar, vinegar, turmeric, celery seed, mustard, and garlic. Add corn. Bring to a full boil. Boil gently for 2 minutes. Remove from heat. Cool slightly. ▼ **Transfer corn** to a moisture- and vapor-proof container. Add enough of the cooking liquid to cover. Cover and chill in the refrigerator for up to 1 week.

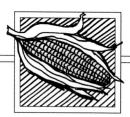

Freezing Corn

To freeze fresh, whole kernel corn, blanch cleaned ears, using 1 gallon of water per pound of vegetables. Blanch for 5 to 6 minutes; cool quickly. Cut corn from cobs at ⅔ depth of kernels; don't scrape. Fill freezer containers, shaking to pack lightly, and leave a ½-inch headspace. Freeze corn up to 10 months.

Southwestern Corn Stuffing

Makes 8 to 10 servings

To make dry bread cubes for this colorful stuffing, cut bread into ½-inch cubes. (Use 16 slices of bread for 8 cups.) Loosely cover bread cubes with a paper towel and let stand at room temperature for 8 to 12 hours.

3 medium ears of fresh corn
▼
1 stalk celery, chopped (½ cup)
1 small green sweet pepper, chopped (½ cup)
1 small red sweet pepper, chopped (½ cup)
1 small onion, chopped (⅓ cup)
1 tablespoon margarine or butter

1 tablespoon snipped fresh cilantro or parsley
¼ teaspoon salt
⅛ teaspoon pepper
▼
8 cups dry whole wheat or white bread cubes
1 to 2 fresh or canned finely chopped jalapeño peppers (2 to 4 tablespoons)
1 to 1¼ cups chicken broth

Per Serving	
Calories	147
Protein	5 g
Carbohydrate	26 g
Total Fat	4 g
Saturated Fat	0 g
Cholesterol	000 mg
Sodium	467 mg
Potassium	215 mg

Remove the husks from corn; scrub with a stiff brush to remove silks. Rinse. Use a sharp knife to cut off just the kernel tips from the ears of corn, then scrape the cobs with the dull edge of the knife. (You should have about 1½ cups.) Cook corn, covered, in a small amount of boiling unsalted water for 2 minutes; drain well. Set aside. ▼ **In a large skillet** cook celery, green and red sweet pepper, and onion in margarine or butter till tender. Stir in cilantro or parsley, salt, and pepper. Set aside. ▼ **In a large mixing bowl** combine cooked corn, bread cubes, and jalapeño pepper. Add celery mixture. Drizzle with enough broth to moisten, tossing lightly. ▼ **Transfer stuffing** to a 2-quart casserole. Bake, covered, in a 375° oven for 30 to 35 minutes or till heated through.

CORN

Maque Choux

Makes 6 servings

Per Serving

Calories	159
Protein	4 g
Carbohydrate	29 g
Total Fat	5 g
Saturated Fat	1 g
Cholesterol	0 mg
Sodium	153 mg
Potassium	349 mg

8 **medium ears of fresh corn**

▼

1 **medium onion, chopped (½ cup)**
1 **small green pepper, chopped (½ cup)**
2 **tablespoons margarine *or* butter**

1 **medium tomato, cut up**
¼ **teaspoon salt**
¼ **teaspoon ground black pepper**
¼ **teaspoon ground red pepper**

Slightly spicy, and a little crunchy, Maque Choux (*MOCK shoo*) is a Cajun smothered corn dish. In Cajun country, smothered means cooked with tomatoes, onion, and green pepper.

Remove the husks from corn; scrub with a stiff brush to remove silks. Rinse. Use a sharp knife to remove corn from cobs, cutting two-thirds of the way to the cob. Scrape cobs with dull edge of a knife. (You should have about 4 cups.) ▼ **In a 3-quart saucepan** cook onion and green pepper in margarine or butter about 5 minutes or till tender. Stir in corn, tomato, salt, black pepper, and red pepper. Cover and cook over low heat about 20 minutes or till corn is tender. Season to taste.

CORN

Corn with Savory-Lime Butter

Makes 4 servings

This recipe doubles easily, so if you're serving real sweet corn fanatics, better plan on more than one ear per person.

4 **medium ears of fresh corn**

▼

¼ **cup butter, softened**

1½ **teaspoons snipped fresh savory or thyme or ½ teaspoon dried savory or thyme, crushed**

½ **teaspoon finely shredded lime peel**

Per Serving

Calories	183
Protein	3 g
Carbohydrate	19 g
Total Fat	12 g
Saturated Fat	7 g
Cholesterol	31 mg
Sodium	129 mg
Potassium	197 mg

Remove the husks from corn; scrub with a stiff brush to remove silks. Rinse. Cook, uncovered, in enough lightly salted boiling water to cover for 5 to 7 minutes or till tender. ▼ **Meanwhile, in a small bowl** thoroughly combine the butter, savory or thyme, and lime peel. Serve herb butter with hot corn. Store any remaining butter, covered, in the refrigerator.

EGGPLANT

Broiled Eggplant

Makes 4 servings

Eggplants look sturdier than they really are— refrigerate them only up to 2 days.

1 **medium eggplant (1 pound)**

▼

2 **tablespoons finely chopped onion**
1 **tablespoon olive oil** *or* **cooking oil**

2 **cloves garlic, minced**

▼

¼ **cup grated Parmesan cheese**
1 **tablespoon snipped fresh basil** *or* **1 teaspoon dried basil, crushed**

Per Serving

Calories	88
Protein	4 g
Carbohydrate	7 g
Total Fat	5 g
Saturated Fat	2 g
Cholesterol	5 mg
Sodium	120 mg
Potassium	251 mg

Wash and peel eggplant; cut crosswise into ½-inch-thick slices. Place eggplant slices on the unheated rack of a broiler pan. ▼ **Combine** onion, olive oil or cooking oil, and garlic; spoon *half* of the onion mixture over the eggplant slices. Broil 4 to 5 inches from heat for 6 minutes; turn. Spoon the remaining onion mixture over eggplant slices. ▼ **Combine** the Parmesan cheese and basil; sprinkle over eggplant slices. Broil for 3 to 5 minutes more or till eggplant is tender.

EGGPLANT

Baked Eggplant

Makes 4 to 6 servings

Per Serving

Calories	314
Protein	9 g
Carbohydrate	14 g
Total Fat	25 g
Saturated Fat	10 g
Cholesterol	42 mg
Sodium	366 mg
Potassium	393 mg

1 medium eggplant
  (1 pound)
  ▼
3 tablespoons margarine *or*
  butter
1 medium green *or* red
  sweet pepper, chopped
  (¾ cup)
2 tablespoons snipped
  fresh basil or 1 teaspoon
  dried basil, crushed
1 clove garlic, minced
2 tablespoons all-purpose
  flour

1 cup half-and-half, light
  cream, *or* milk
¼ cup grated Parmesan
  cheese
1 tablespoon dry white
  wine
½ cup shredded cheddar
  cheese (2 ounces)
  ▼
2 tablespoons snipped
  parsley

A rich, cheesy sauce smothers the eggplant slices in this easy, summertime side dish.

Wash and peel eggplant; cut crosswise into ½-inch-thick slices. ▼ **In a large skillet** cook eggplant, half at a time, in *2 tablespoons* of the margarine or butter for 4 to 6 minutes or till lightly browned, turning once. (Add more margarine or butter if necessary.) Place eggplant slices in an 8x8x2-inch baking dish. In the same skillet cook sweet pepper, basil, and garlic in the remaining 1 tablespoon margarine or butter till pepper is tender. Stir in flour. Add half-and-half, light cream, or milk all at once. Cook and stir till thickened and bubbly. Stir in the Parmesan cheese and wine. Pour over eggplant slices in dish. Sprinkle cheddar cheese on top. ▼ **Bake,** uncovered, in a 350° oven about 15 minutes or till hot and cheese is melted. Sprinkle with parsley.

EGGPLANT

Caponata

Makes 8 to 10 appetizer servings (about 3½ cups)

To serve this tangy Sicilian antipasto, spoon the mixture onto the pita triangles or chunks of French bread.

1 medium onion, sliced and separated into rings
¼ cup sliced celery
1 tablespoon olive oil or salad oil
1 medium eggplant (1 pound), peeled and cut into ½-inch cubes (about 4 cups)
1 medium yellow summer squash, cut into ½-inch cubes (about 1¼ cups)
1 small tomato, peeled, seeded, and chopped (½ cup)

2 tablespoons halved pimiento-stuffed olives
2 tablespoons red wine vinegar
1 tablespoon capers, rinsed and drained
1 tablespoon raisins (optional)
1 teaspoon sugar
▼
1 tablespoon pine nuts *or* slivered almonds (optional)

Per Serving

Calories	52
Protein	1 g
Carbohydrate	7 g
Total Fat	3 g
Saturated Fat	0 g
Cholesterol	0 mg
Sodium	66 mg
Potassium	227 mg

In a large skillet cook onion and celery in hot oil till tender. Add eggplant, squash, tomato, olives, vinegar, capers, raisins (if desired), and sugar; stir to combine. ▼ **Simmer mixture,** covered, for 8 to 10 minutes or till eggplant and squash are tender. Simmer, uncovered, for 5 to 10 minutes more or till most of the liquid has evaporated. Season to taste with salt and pepper. Cool slightly. ▼ **Add pine nuts,** if desired. Cool and serve at room temperature. (Or, cover and chill overnight. Let stand at room temperature before serving.)

ZUCCHINI

Zucchini Chocolate Cake

Makes 12 servings

Per Serving

Calories	361
Protein	5 g
Carbohydrate	43 g
Total Fat	19 g
Saturated Fat	3 g
Cholesterol	36 mg
Sodium	232 mg
Potassium	110 mg

2½ cups all-purpose flour
1⅓ cups sugar
⅓ cup unsweetened cocoa powder
1 teaspoon baking soda
½ teaspoon baking powder
½ teaspoon ground cinnamon
¼ teaspoon salt
½ cup cooking oil

½ cup milk
½ cup margarine or butter, softened
1 teaspoon vanilla
2 eggs
2 medium zucchini, shredded (2 cups)
▼
Sifted powdered sugar

Got a garden full of zucchini? Put some in this super-moist chocolate cake and no one will be the wiser.

Grease and flour a 13x9x2-inch baking pan; set aside. ▼ **In a large mixing bowl** combine flour, sugar, cocoa powder, baking soda, baking powder, cinnamon, and salt. Add oil, milk, margarine or butter, and vanilla. Beat with an electric mixer on low speed till combined. Add eggs and shredded zucchini and beat on medium to high speed for 2 minutes. ▼ **Spread batter** into prepared pan. Bake in a 350° oven about 35 minutes or till cake tests done. Let cake cool in the pan on a wire rack. Sprinkle with powdered sugar.

ZUCCHINI

Summer Squash au Gratin

Makes 4 servings

Besides the slender, green-skinned zucchini we're all familiar with, there is also a golden or yellow zucchini available. Yellow summer squash is available in crookneck and straight-neck varieties.

2 medium zucchini *and/or* yellow summer squash, sliced (2½ cups)

▼

1 tablespoon margarine *or* butter
2 teaspoons all-purpose flour
⅛ teaspoon pepper
½ cup milk
½ cup shredded Gruyère cheese (2 ounces)

¼ cup crumbled feta cheese (1 ounce)
2 green onions, thinly sliced (¼ cup)

▼

¼ cup fine dry bread crumbs
1 tablespoon snipped parsley
1 tablespoon margarine *or* butter, melted

Per Serving

Calories	182
Protein	8 g
Carbohydrate	10 g
Total Fat	13 g
Saturated Fat	5 g
Cholesterol	24 mg
Sodium	255 mg
Potassium	177 mg

Cook zucchini and/or yellow summer squash, covered, in a small amount of boiling salted water for 3 to 5 minutes or till crisp-tender. Drain well. ▼ **In a medium saucepan** melt 1 tablespoon margarine or butter. Stir in the flour and pepper. Add milk all at once. Cook and stir till thickened and bubbly. Cook and stir for 1 minute more. Add the Gruyère and feta cheeses, stirring till almost melted. Stir in the cooked zucchini and green onion. ▼ **Transfer to** a 1-quart casserole. Combine bread crumbs, parsley, and 1 tablespoon melted margarine or butter. Sprinkle over zucchini mixture. Bake in a 350° oven for 20 to 25 minutes or till crumbs brown slightly.

Zucchini-Basil Salad Dressing

Makes about 1 cup (sixteen 1-tablespoon servings)

A thick, tangy dressing that clings well to salad greens.

Per Serving

Calories	59
Protein	0 g
Carbohydrate	1 g
Total Fat	6 g
Saturated Fat	1 g
Cholesterol	6 mg
Sodium	43 mg
Potassium	23 mg

1 small zucchini, coarsely chopped (¾ cup)
½ cup mayonnaise or salad dressing
¼ cup dairy sour cream
2 tablespoons buttermilk
1 tablespoon snipped fresh basil *or* 1 teaspoon dried basil, crushed

¼ teaspoon garlic powder
¼ teaspoon onion powder
¼ teaspoon pepper
¼ cup finely chopped zucchini (optional)

In a blender container or food processor bowl combine the ¾ cup chopped zucchini, mayonnaise or salad dressing, sour cream, buttermilk, basil, garlic powder, onion powder, and pepper. Cover and blend or process till mixture is almost smooth. Stir in the ¼ cup chopped zucchini, if desired. Cover and store in the refrigerator for up to 1 week.

Sautéed Zucchini And Apples

Makes 4 servings

The perfect accompaniment to grilled pork chops.

1 medium onion, cut into
   thin wedges (1 cup)
½ teaspoon grated
   gingerroot
2 tablespoons margarine or
   butter

▼

2 medium zucchini or
   yellow summer squash,
   cut into ¼-inch-thick
   slices (2½ cups)
1 medium cooking apple,
   cored and thinly sliced
   (1 cup)

Per Serving

Calories	88
Protein	1 g
Carbohydrate	9 g
Total Fat	6 g
Saturated Fat	1 g
Cholesterol	0 mg
Sodium	68 mg
Potassium	167 mg

Cook onion and grated gingerroot, covered, in margarine or butter over low heat about 20 minutes or till very tender, stirring occasionally. Uncover and cook over medium-high heat about 10 minutes more or till onions are a deep golden color, stirring frequently. ▼ **Add the zucchini** or yellow summer squash and apple, stirring gently to coat. Cover and cook for 3 to 5 minutes more or till zucchini and apple are just tender, stirring often.

Herbed Summer Salad

Makes 6 servings

If you've got cherry tomatoes on hand, halve them and use them instead of the small tomato wedges called for.

¼ **cup salad oil**
3 **tablespoons white wine vinegar**
1 **green onion, thinly sliced (2 tablespoons)**
2 **tablespoons snipped parsley**
2 **tablespoons mayonnaise or salad dressing**
1 **tablespoon snipped fresh basil or ½ teaspoon dried basil, crushed**
1 **tablespoon snipped fresh dill or ½ teaspoon dried dillweed**

1 **teaspoon snipped fresh oregano or ¼ teaspoon dried oregano, crushed**
¼ **teaspoon salt**
⅛ **teaspoon pepper**
1 **clove garlic, minced**
▼
2 **medium yellow summer squash *or* zucchini, cut into ¼-inch-thick slices (2½ cups)**
2 **small tomatoes, cut into wedges**
1 **cup sliced mushrooms**
Lettuce leaves

Per Serving

Calories	137
Protein	2 g
Carbohydrate	5 g
Total Fat	13 g
Saturated Fat	2 g
Cholesterol	3 mg
Sodium	123 mg
Potassium	319 mg

For dressing, in a screw-top jar combine oil, vinegar, green onion, parsley, mayonnaise or salad dressing, basil, dill, oregano, salt, pepper, and garlic. Cover and shake well. Set dressing aside. ▼ **In a large mixing bowl** combine yellow summer squash or zucchini, tomato wedges, and mushrooms. Pour dressing over all. Stir gently to coat. Transfer to a lettuce-lined salad bowl.

SUMMER SQUASH

Stuffed Miniature Squash

Makes 16 to 20 appetizers

Per Serving

Calories	46
Protein	1 g
Carbohydrate	3 g
Total Fat	4 g
Saturated Fat	1 g
Cholesterol	0 mg
Sodium	67 mg
Potassium	207 mg

16 to 20 baby zucchini *or*
    baby yellow
    sunburst squash
▼
2 ripe avocados, seeded,
    peeled, and cut up

2 tablespoons lemon juice
1 tablespoon snipped fresh
    basil *or* 1 teaspoon dried
    basil, crushed
½ teaspoon garlic salt
¼ teaspoon pepper

In a large saucepan cook baby zucchini and/or sunburst squash, covered, in a small amount of boiling water for 2 to 3 minutes or till crisp-tender. Drain; chill squash till cool. **For zucchini,** cut each in half lengthwise. With a small spoon, scoop out most of the flesh from each zucchini, leaving a ¼-inch-thick shell. **For sunburst squash,** using a knife or apple corer, cut around stem. With a spoon, remove stem and hollow out as much of the flesh as you can, working from the hole in the top of the squash (do not break through the bottom skin).

▼ **For filling,** in a blender container or food processor bowl combine avocados, lemon juice, basil, garlic salt, and pepper. Cover and blend or process till smooth. Using a pastry bag fitted with a large star tip, pipe filling down the center of the zucchini or sunburst squash cavity. (Or, just spoon filling in each.) Serve immediately. (The filling darkens upon standing.)

If baby vegetables are unavailable, use 8 small zucchini and increase the cooking time to 5 minutes. Cut and scoop out each zucchini as directed, except cut the squash in half crosswise before filling (to make 4 appetizers per zucchini).

SWEET PEPPERS

Roasted Sweet Pepper Tart

Makes 12 appetizer servings

The filling for this rich, delectable appetizer tart mixes goat cheese, prosciutto, and dry white wine with a roasted sweet pepper.

1 **large red sweet pepper**

▼

½ **of an 11-ounce package (1⅓ cups) piecrust mix**

▼

8 **ounces chèvre cheese (goat's cheese)**

½ **cup half-and-half or light cream**

3 **eggs**

¼ **cup dry white wine**

2 **ounces lean prosciutto *or* Canadian-style bacon, finely chopped**

▼

Fresh chives *or* green onion tops (optional)

Fresh basil leaves (optional)

Per Serving

Calories	182
Protein	7 g
Carbohydrate	8 g
Total Fat	13 g
Saturated Fat	5 g
Cholesterol	66 mg
Sodium	266 mg
Potassium	57 mg

To roast pepper, quarter pepper lengthwise. Remove stem and seeds. Cut small slits into ends of pepper pieces to make them lie flat. Place pepper pieces, cut sides down, on foil-lined baking sheet. Bake in a 425° oven 20 to 25 minutes or till skins are bubbly. Immediately place pepper pieces in a clean brown paper bag. Close bag tightly; cool. Cut *one-fourth* of the roasted pepper into strips; reserve. Chop remaining roasted pepper; set aside. ▼ **Meanwhile, prepare pastry** according to package directions. Roll piecrust into a 13x10-inch rectangle or a 12-inch circle. Ease rectangular piecrust into an 11x8x1-inch tart pan with a removable bottom. For round piecrust, ease pastry into a 10-inch tart pan with a removable bottom. To trim away excess dough, use your fingers or a rolling pin to press excess dough against pan edge; remove and discard excess dough. Line piecrust with a double thickness of foil. Bake in a 425° oven 5 minutes. Remove foil. Bake 5 to 7 minutes more or till pastry is nearly done. ▼ **For filling,** beat chèvre cheese, half-and-half or light cream, and eggs with an electric mixer till smooth. Stir in wine. Add chopped roasted pepper and prosciutto, mixing well. Pour filling into baked piecrust on an oven rack. Decorate with reserved roasted pepper strips. (For roasted pepper flowers, if desired, place pepper strips in flowerlike designs, leaving room for chives or onion greens for flower stems and basil for flower leaves after baking.) ▼ **Reduce oven temperature** to 375°. Bake 20 to 25 minutes for rectangular tart (30 to 35 minutes for round tart) or till a knife inserted near center comes out clean. Let cool 15 minutes on a rack.

SWEET PEPPERS

Peppered Pizza Appetizer

Makes 16 appetizer servings

Per Serving

Calories	136
Protein	4 g
Carbohydrate	14 g
Total Fat	7 g
Saturated Fat	1 g
Cholesterol	4 mg
Sodium	205 mg
Potassium	60 mg

2 **cloves garlic, minced**
¼ **cup chopped onion**
1 **tablespoon olive oil or cooking oil**
⅓ **cup dry white wine**
1 **tablespoon snipped fresh basil or 1 teaspoon dried basil, crushed**
▼
2 **medium red sweet peppers, chopped (2 cups)**
1 **tablespoon olive oil *or* cooking oil**

2 **medium yellow or green sweet peppers, cut into julienne strips (2 cups)**
1 **tablespoon olive oil *or* cooking oil**
▼
1 **16-ounce Italian bread shell (Boboli)**
½ **cup crumbled Gorgonzola cheese *or* blue cheese (2 ounces)**

If you're a blue cheese fan, you might want to go up to 3 ounces. If you're not, substitute mozzarella or provolone cheese.

In a small skillet cook garlic and onion in 1 tablespoon hot olive oil or cooking oil till onion is tender but not brown. Stir in the white wine and basil. Reduce heat and cook, uncovered, about 3 minutes or till most of the liquid has evaporated. Set aside. ▼ **In a large skillet** cook chopped red sweet pepper in 1 tablespoon hot olive oil or cooking oil about 10 minutes or till tender. Remove red pepper. In same skillet cook yellow or green sweet pepper strips in 1 tablespoon olive oil about 5 minutes or just till softened. Remove pepper strips from the skillet. ▼ **For sauce,** in a blender container or food processor bowl combine the onion mixture and the cooked red pepper. Cover and blend or process till nearly smooth, stopping and scraping sides as necessary. ▼ **To assemble,** place Italian bread shell on a baking sheet. Spread sauce over crust. Sprinkle Gorgonzola cheese or blue cheese over sauce. Arrange yellow or green sweet pepper strips over cheese. Bake in a 400° oven about 10 minutes or till hot. To serve, cut into wedges.

SWEET PEPPERS

Turkey-Stuffed Peppers

Makes 4 main-dish servings

Top these colorful stuffed peppers with any cheese you like— from mild American to lively hot pepper.

2 **large sweet peppers (yellow, red, *or* green)**

▼

¾ **pound ground turkey**
1 **medium leek, thinly sliced (⅓ cup)**
1 **clove garlic, minced**
2 **medium tomatoes, chopped (1½ cups)**
1 **cup sliced mushrooms**
¾ **cup quick-cooking rice**
¼ **cup water**
1 **tablespoon snipped parsley**

1 **tablespoon snipped fresh basil or ¾ teaspoon dried basil, crushed**
1 **teaspoon instant chicken bouillon granules**
Few dashes bottled hot pepper sauce

▼

1 **slice Colby cheese (1 ounce), cut into 4 triangles**

Per Serving

Calories	310
Protein	17 g
Carbohydrate	40 g
Total Fat	9 g
Saturated Fat	3 g
Cholesterol	38 mg
Sodium	309 mg
Potassium	501 mg

Halve peppers lengthwise; discard seeds and membrane. Cook peppers, uncovered, in boiling water for 3 to 5 minutes; invert on paper towels to drain well. ▼ **In a skillet** cook ground turkey, leek, and garlic till no pink remains in turkey, and leek is tender. Drain off any fat. Stir in chopped tomatoes, mushrooms, *uncooked* rice, water, parsley, basil, bouillon granules, and hot pepper sauce. Bring to boiling; reduce heat. Cover and simmer about 15 minutes or till rice is tender. Place pepper halves in an 8x8x2-inch baking dish. Fill each pepper half with some of the turkey-rice mixture. ▼ **Bake,** covered, in a 350° oven for 30 to 35 minutes or till heated through. Top each pepper with a cheese triangle. Serve immediately.

PEPPERS

Casserole-Style Chiles Rellenos

Makes 4 main-dish servings

This is a streamlined version of the classic Chiles Rellenos (*CHEE-lehs reh-YEH-nohs*). Instead of dipping stuffed chilies in batter and frying, we layered them in a baking dish and poured the batter over the top— less work and less mess, but equally as delicious.

2 large poblano peppers *or* green sweet peppers (8 ounces)
1 cup shredded Monterey Jack cheese with jalapeño peppers (4 ounces)
▼
3 beaten eggs
¼ cup milk

⅓ cup all-purpose flour
½ teaspoon baking powder
¼ teaspoon ground red pepper
⅛ teaspoon salt
▼
¾ cup shredded cheddar cheese (3 ounces)
1 cup picante sauce
¼ cup dairy sour cream

Per Serving

Calories	352
Protein	20 g
Carbohydrate	17 g
Total Fat	24 g
Saturated Fat	13 g
Cholesterol	215 mg
Sodium	891 mg
Potassium	382 mg

Quarter the peppers and remove stems, seeds, and veins. Immerse peppers into boiling water for 3 minutes. Drain. Invert on paper towels to drain well. Place *half* the peppers in a well-greased 1½-quart casserole. Top with *half* of the shredded Monterey Jack cheese. Repeat layers. ▼ **In a medium mixing bowl** combine eggs and milk. Add flour, baking powder, red pepper, and salt. Beat till smooth. Pour egg mixture over peppers. ▼ **Bake,** uncovered, in a 450° oven for 15 minutes or till set. Sprinkle with the shredded cheddar cheese. Let stand about 5 minutes or till cheese melts. Serve with picante sauce and sour cream.

Jalapeño Quiche
With Red Salsa

Makes 6 servings

Per Serving

Calories	400
Protein	16 g
Carbohydrate	27 g
Total Fat	26 g
Saturated Fat	10 g
Cholesterol	141 mg
Sodium	573 mg
Potassium	330 mg

Pastry for Single-Crust Pie (see recipe, page 163)

▼

- 3 **beaten eggs**
- 1½ **cups milk**
- 1 **small red sweet pepper, chopped (½ cup)**
- ¼ **cup sliced pitted ripe olives**
- 2 **green onions, thinly sliced (¼ cup)**
- 1 **to 2 fresh *or* canned jalapeño peppers, seeded and chopped (2 to 4 tablespoons)**
- ⅛ **teaspoon salt**
- ⅛ **teaspoon pepper**
- 1½ **cups shredded cheddar cheese (6 ounces)**
- 1 **tablespoon all-purpose flour**

▼

Red Salsa

Jalapeño peppers are short, plump, little barrels with a thick, green to reddish green skin. They range from hot to very hot. Jalapeños are probably the most available of all fresh hot peppers.

Prepare Pastry for Single-Crust Pie. Ease pastry into a 10-inch tart pan with a removable bottom or a 10- inch quiche dish. Press pastry into fluted sides of tart pan or quiche dish and trim edges. Line unpricked pastry shell with a double thickness of foil. Bake in a 450° oven 8 minutes. Remove foil. Bake 4 to 5 minutes more or till pastry is set and dry. Remove from oven. Reduce oven temperature to 325°. ▼ **Meanwhile, in a large bowl** stir together eggs, milk, red sweet pepper, olives, green onion, jalapeño pepper, salt, and pepper. In a medium bowl, toss together shredded cheese and flour. Sprinkle cheese mixture over bottom of *hot* pastry shell. Carefully pour egg mixture into pastry shell.
▼ **Bake** in 325° oven 35 to 40 minutes or till a knife inserted near the center comes out clean. If necessary, cover edge of crust with foil to prevent overbrowning. Let stand 10 minutes. Serve with Red Salsa.

Red Salsa

In a small mixing bowl combine 1 large *tomato,* finely chopped (1¼ cups); 1 small *onion,* chopped (⅓ cup); 1 *tomatillo,* finely chopped (about ¼ cup); 1 *jalapeño pepper,* finely chopped (2 tablespoons); 1 tablespoon snipped fresh *cilantro;* 1 to 2 teaspoons *lime juice;* ¼ teaspoon *salt;* and 1 clove *garlic,* minced. Stir gently to mix. Cover and refrigerate for 1 hour before serving. Cover any leftover salsa and store in the refrigerator for up to 1 week. Makes about 2 cups.

SWEET PEPPERS

Yellow Pepper and Red Tomato Salad

Makes 4 to 6 servings

Summer eating at its best—ripe, juicy tomatoes and crisp peppers, accented with a hint of Dijon-style mustard and blue-veined cheese.

2 tablespoons olive oil *or* salad oil

2 tablespoons white wine vinegar

1 tablespoon thinly sliced green onion *or* snipped fresh chives

2 teaspoons snipped fresh basil or ½ teaspoon dried basil, crushed

1 teaspoon sugar

½ teaspoon Dijon-style mustard

⅛ teaspoon pepper

▼

3 large yellow sweet peppers, thinly sliced into rings (about 3 cups)

▼

3 large red tomatoes, sliced Spinach leaves

⅔ cup crumbled Gorgonzola cheese *or* blue cheese (3 ounces)

Per Serving

Calories	182
Protein	7 g
Carbohydrate	12 g
Total Fat	13 g
Saturated Fat	5 g
Cholesterol	16 mg
Sodium	331 mg
Potassium	509 mg

For dressing, in a screw-top jar combine olive oil or salad oil, vinegar, green onion or chives, basil, sugar, mustard, and pepper. Cover and shake well. Chill, if desired. ▼ **In a skillet** cook sweet pepper rings, covered, in a small amount of boiling water for 1 to 2 minutes or just till crisp-tender; drain and cool. Chill, if desired. ▼ **To serve,** arrange tomato slices and sweet pepper rings on a spinach-lined platter. Sprinkle crumbled cheese atop salad. Shake dressing well; drizzle atop salad.

HOT PEPPERS

Western-Style Pepper Jelly

Makes about 5 half-pints (eighty 1-tablespoon servings)

Spoon this spunky jelly atop corn bread muffins or brush over chicken while grilling or roasting.

2 **medium cooking apples,**
   cored and coarsely
   chopped (2 cups)
1 **medium green sweet**
   pepper coarsely
   chopped (¾ cup)
6 **to 8 jalapeño peppers,**
   halved
5 **cups sugar**
1½ **cups cider vinegar**

▼
½ **of a 6-ounce package**
   (1 foil pouch) liquid
   fruit pectin
¼ **cup finely chopped green**
   sweet pepper
¼ **cup finely chopped red**
   sweet pepper
1 **small banana pepper,**
   finely chopped

Per Serving

Calories	47
Protein	0 g
Carbohydrate	13 g
Total Fat	0 g
Saturated Fat	0 g
Cholesterol	0 mg
Sodium	0 mg
Potassium	15 mg

In a 4- or 5-quart Dutch oven combine apples, green pepper, jalapeño peppers, sugar, vinegar, and ¼ cup *water*. Bring to boiling; reduce heat. Boil gently, uncovered, for 10 minutes. Strain mixture through a sieve, pressing with back of a spoon to remove all liquid (you should have about 4 cups). Discard pulp. ▼ **Return liquid** to Dutch oven; bring to boil. Add pectin; bring to a full, rolling boil. Boil hard for 1 minute, stirring occasionally. Remove from heat. Stir in finely chopped green and red sweet pepper and banana pepper. ▼ **Pour into** hot, sterilized half-pint jars, leaving ¼-inch headspace. Wipe rims; adjust lids. Process in boiling-water canner for 5 minutes (start timing after water boils). Remove and cool on wire rack till set (jelly will take 2 to 3 days to set). Note: Chopped pepper pieces will float to top on standing.

Handle With Care

When seeding and chopping hot peppers such as the jalapeños in the recipe above, protect your hands with rubber gloves because the oils in the peppers can irritate your skin. Also, be careful not to touch or rub your eyes. When you're done handling the hot peppers, wash your hands and nails well with soap and water.

JICAMA

Mexican-Style Pickled Peppers and Jicama

Makes 4 pints (16 servings)

½ **pound banana peppers**
1½ **pounds jicama**
8 **cups water**
¼ **cup pickling salt**

▼
2 **cups vinegar**
4 **teaspoons dried basil, crushed**
4 *or* **5 cloves garlic**

Use only pickling salt when preparing this zippy condiment. Regular table salt clouds the pickling liquid.

Slice peppers crosswise into ½- inch strips; rinse. Discard seeds and any interior pulp. Peel and slice jicama lengthwise into 4-inch sticks. Combine *4 cups* of the water and the salt. In a large bowl cover the peppers and the jicama with the salt solution. Let vegetables stand overnight. Drain and rinse well. ▼ **In a large saucepan** combine the remaining 4 cups water, the vinegar, and the basil. Bring mixture to boiling; simmer, uncovered, for 10 minutes. Pack the peppers and jicama loosely into 4 hot, sterilized pint jars, leaving ½-inch headspace. Add a clove of garlic to each jar. Pour the hot vinegar solution over peppers and jicama, just to cover, stirring solution to keep herbs evenly distributed. Leave ½-inch headspace in each pint jar. Wipe rims and adjust lids. Process in a boiling-water canner for 10 minutes. (Begin timing when water boils.)

Note: Nutrition analysis was determined by assuming that half the salt is rinsed off the chilled vegetable mixture before processing.

CAULIFLOWER

Party Vegetable Platter

Makes 6 servings

In springtime, when asparagus is plentiful, substitute it for the green beans. You'll need to use about ¾ pound of asparagus spears.

1 head cauliflower
  (about 1½ pounds)
  ▼
½ pound green beans
  ▼
¼ cup white wine vinegar
3 tablespoons Dijon-style
  mustard
1 tablespoon sugar

⅓ cup olive oil or salad oil
  ▼
Leaf lettuce
Cherry tomatoes, halved
Pitted ripe olives
Lemon slices, halved
  (optional)
Fresh thyme (optional)

Per Serving

Calories	175
Protein	4 g
Carbohydrate	12 g
Total Fat	14 g
Saturated Fat	2 g
Cholesterol	0 mg
Sodium	227 mg
Potassium	532 mg

Wash cauliflower and remove leaves and woody stem. Break into flowerets. (You should have about 4 cups.) ▼ **Place a steamer** basket in a saucepan. Add water to just below the bottom of the steamer basket. Bring to boiling. Add green beans. Steam, covered, for 18 to 22 minutes or till crisp-tender. Remove green beans from steamer basket; chill till serving time. ▼ **Add water** to just below the bottom of the steamer basket, if necessary. Return to boiling. Add cauliflower. Steam, covered, for 8 to 12 minutes or till crisp-tender. Remove cauliflower from steamer basket; chill till serving time. ▼ **For dressing,** in a blender container or food processor bowl combine vinegar, mustard, and sugar. Cover and blend for 5 seconds. With blender running slowly, add oil in a thin, steady stream through the opening in the lid. (When necessary, stop blender or food processor and use a rubber scraper to scrape sides.) Season to taste with salt and pepper. Cover and chill till serving time. ▼ **To serve,** arrange green beans on one side of a large platter. Line remaining half of the platter with lettuce. Arrange cauliflower on top of the lettuce. Add several cherry tomatoes and ripe olives. Drizzle vegetables with the dressing. Garnish the platter with lemon slices and thyme, if desired.

CAULIFLOWER

Creamy Cauliflower Bake

Makes 4 servings

Per Serving

Calories	270
Protein	9 g
Carbohydrate	13 g
Total Fat	21 g
Saturated Fat	9 g
Cholesterol	37 mg
Sodium	320 mg
Potassium	480 mg

1 **head cauliflower (about 1½ pounds)**
  ▼
1 **small onion, chopped (⅓ cup)**
2 **tablespoons margarine or butter**
2 **tablespoons all-purpose flour**
¼ **teaspoon salt**
⅛ **to ¼ teaspoon pepper**

Dash ground red pepper
1 **cup half-and-half, light cream, or milk**
½ **cup shredded cheddar or American cheese (2 ounces)**
¼ **cup slivered almonds**
  ▼
2 **tablespoons snipped parsley**

Serve this cheesy vegetable dish with grilled steak or hamburgers.

Wash cauliflower and remove leaves and woody stem. Break into flowerets. (You should have about 4 cups.) In a medium saucepan cook cauliflower, covered, in a small amount of boiling salted water for 5 minutes. Drain. ▼ **In the same saucepan** cook onion in margarine or butter till onion is tender but not brown. Stir in the flour, salt, pepper, and ground red pepper. Add half-and-half, light cream, or milk all at once. Cook and stir over medium heat till thickened and bubbly. Add cheese, stirring till cheese melts. Stir in cooked cauliflower. Transfer mixture to a 1-quart casserole. Sprinkle with almonds. ▼ **Bake** in a 350° oven about 15 minutes or till heated through. Sprinkle the top with the snipped parsley.

Indian Cauliflower

Makes 4 servings

Place any extra cauliflower in a plastic bag and store in the refrigerator for up to 4 days.

1 **head cauliflower (about 1½ pounds)**
▼
1 **tablespoon cooking oil**
4 **green onions, bias sliced into 1-inch pieces (¾ cup)**
1 **small red sweet pepper, cut into 1-inch squares (½ cup)**

½ **teaspoon dry mustard**
¼ **teaspoon ground turmeric**
¼ **teaspoon ground cumin**
⅛ **teaspoon ground coriander**
⅛ **teaspoon ground red pepper**
¼ **cup chicken broth**

Per Serving

Calories	71
Protein	3 g
Carbohydrate	7 g
Total Fat	4 g
Saturated Fat	1 g
Cholesterol	0 mg
Sodium	58 mg
Potassium	463 mg

Wash cauliflower and remove leaves and woody stem. Break into flowerets. (You should have about 4 cups.) In a medium saucepan cook cauliflower, covered, in a small amount of boiling salted water for 5 minutes. Drain. ▼ **Pour cooking oil** into a wok or a large skillet. (Add more oil as necessary during cooking.) Preheat over medium-high heat. Add the green onion and red sweet pepper; stir-fry for 1 to 1½ minutes. Reduce heat to medium. Add mustard, turmeric, cumin, coriander, and ground red pepper. Cook and stir for 30 seconds. Add chicken broth and cooked cauliflower. Stir all ingredients together to coat. Cook and stir about 1 minute more or till heated through. Serve immediately.

CAULIFLOWER

Cauliflower-Cilantro Salad

Makes 6 to 8 servings

Per Serving

Calories	110
Protein	3 g
Carbohydrate	6 g
Total Fat	9 g
Saturated Fat	2 g
Cholesterol	4 mg
Sodium	80 mg
Potassium	328 mg

1 head cauliflower
   (about 1½ pounds)
1 small red onion, thinly
   sliced and separated
   into rings
   ▼
3 tablespoons salad oil
3 tablespoons white wine
   vinegar *or* vinegar

2 tablespoons snipped
   fresh cilantro *or* parsley
½ teaspoon sugar
1 clove garlic, minced
   ▼
1 medium tomato, cut
   into wedges
4 slices bacon, crisp-
   cooked, drained, and
   crumbled

A perfect summer side dish with a fresh, crisp flavor.

Wash cauliflower and remove leaves and woody stem. Break into flowerets. (You should have about 4 cups.) In a medium saucepan cook cauliflower, covered, in a small amount of boiling salted water for 2 minutes. Drain. In a large salad bowl combine cooked cauliflower and onion rings. Set aside. ▼ **For the dressing,** in a screw-top jar combine salad oil, vinegar, cilantro or parsley, sugar, and garlic. Cover and shake well. Pour dressing over cauliflower mixture. Toss lightly to coat. Cover and chill for 4 to 24 hours. ▼ **Before serving,** add tomato wedges; toss lightly. Sprinkle with crumbled bacon.

OKRA

Fried Okra with Cheese Sauce

Makes 8 to 10 appetizer servings

Fresh okra is available in the South throughout the year, and is most plentiful in other parts of the country July through September.

2   green onions, cut into ½-inch pieces
1   tablespoon margarine *or* butter
1   large tomato, peeled, seeded, and chopped (¾ cup)
1   fresh or canned jalapeño pepper, seeded and chopped (2 tablespoons)
1   8-ounce package cheese spread, chopped (Velveeta)

▼

½   pound small whole okra (36 to 40)
¼   cup all-purpose flour
¼   cup yellow cornmeal
½   teaspoon ground red pepper
¼   teaspoon salt
1   slightly beaten egg
1   tablespoon milk

▼

Shortening *or* cooking oil for deep-fat frying

Per Serving

Calories	222
Protein	7 g
Carbohydrate	12 g
Total Fat	17 g
Saturated Fat	6 g
Cholesterol	43 mg
Sodium	477 mg
Potassium	229 mg

For cheese sauce, in a saucepan cook green onion in margarine or butter till tender. Stir in chopped tomato and jalapeño pepper. Bring to boiling, stirring constantly. Gradually add cheese to saucepan, stirring till melted. Keep warm. ▼ **Wash okra** and cut off stems; set aside. In a plastic bag combine flour, cornmeal, red pepper, and salt. In a small mixing bowl combine egg and milk. Toss okra in egg mixture. Add *one-fourth* of the okra to the plastic bag, closing bag and shaking to coat okra well. Repeat with remaining okra. ▼ **Fry okra,** a few at a time, in deep, hot fat (375°) for 3 to 4 minutes or till golden, turning once. Remove from oil; drain on paper towels. Serve warm with cheese sauce.

Dill-Pickled Okra

Makes 6 pints (36 servings)

Per Serving

Calories	7
Protein	0 g
Carbohydrate	2 g
Total Fat	0 g
Saturated Fat	0 g
Cholesterol	0 mg
Sodium	179 mg
Potassium	67 mg

2½ **pounds small whole okra**
▼
3 **cups cider vinegar**
2 **tablespoons pickling salt**
6 **cloves garlic**

1 **tablespoon mustard seed**
12 **heads fresh dill** *or*
 3 **tablespoons dillseed**
1½ **teaspoons crushed red**
 pepper

Southern cooks often pickle the excess okra from their gardens.

Wash okra and cut off stems. Set aside. ▼ **In a saucepan** mix vinegar, salt, and 2 cups *water*. Bring to boiling. Keep warm over low heat. In each of six hot, sterilized pint jars, place *1 clove* garlic, *½ teaspoon* mustard seed, *2 heads* fresh dill or *1½ teaspoons* dillseed, and *¼ teaspoon* crushed red pepper. ▼ **Immediately** pack okra loosely into the jars, standing okra upright and leaving a ½-inch headspace. Pour hot vinegar mixture over okra maintaining the ½-inch headspace. Wipe rims and adjust lids. Process in a boiling-water canner for 10 minutes. (Begin timing when water boils.) Let stand 1 week before opening.

Farmer's Market Tips

Don't go overboard! Everything at a farmer's market looks so tempting, you can easily buy more than you can use. Remember how much refrigerator space you have at home and have a good idea what groceries you'll need for the week ahead.

If you plan to can or freeze any fruits and vegetables, consider purchasing slightly imperfect ones. You may even be able to barter with a farmer over bruised produce, especially if it's late in the day.

Skillet Okra And Vegetables

Makes 4 servings

When cooked, okra develops a slippery quality (called ropy) that thickens any liquid in which it is cooked.

1 medium green sweet pepper, chopped (¾ cup)
1 medium onion, chopped (½ cup)
2 cloves garlic, minced
2 tablespoons margarine *or* butter
2 large tomatoes, peeled and chopped (2½ cups)

½ pound okra, cut into ½-inch-thick pieces (2 cups)
1 cup cut fresh corn
¼ teaspoon salt
⅛ teaspoon paprika
⅛ teaspoon ground red pepper
3 slices bacon, crisp-cooked, drained, and crumbled

Per Serving

Calories	189
Protein	6 g
Carbohydrate	25 g
Total Fat	9 g
Saturated Fat	2 g
Cholesterol	4 mg
Sodium	531 mg
Potassium	783 mg

In a large skillet cook green pepper, onion, and garlic in margarine or butter till onion is tender but not brown. Stir in the tomatoes, okra, corn, salt, paprika, and red pepper. Cook, covered, over medium-low heat about 20 minutes or till okra is tender. Sprinkle with crumbled bacon.

Lemon-Broccoli Rice

Makes 4 servings

A great side
dish for grilled
or roasted
chicken.

¾ **pound broccoli**

▼

½ **cup long grain rice**
1 **medium onion, chopped**
  (½ cup)
2 **tablespoons margarine** *or*
  butter

1 **cup chicken broth**
1 **8-ounce can sliced water**
  chestnuts, drained
⅓ **cup water**
1 **teaspoon finely shredded**
  lemon peel
¼ **teaspoon lemon-pepper**
  seasoning

Per Serving

Calories	204
Protein	7 g
Carbohydrate	31 g
Total Fat	7 g
Saturated Fat	1 g
Cholesterol	0 mg
Sodium	499 mg
Potassium	500 mg

Wash broccoli; remove outer leaves and tough parts of broccoli stalks. Cut into ½-inch pieces. (You should have about 3 cups.) Cook broccoli, covered, in a small amount of boiling salted water for 8 to 12 minutes or till crisp-tender; drain. ▼ **In a medium saucepan** cook the rice and onion in margarine or butter till onion is tender but not brown. Remove from the heat. Stir in the broth, water chestnuts, water, lemon peel, and lemon-pepper seasoning. Bring to boiling; reduce heat. Cover and simmer about 15 minutes or till rice is tender. Stir in the cooked broccoli. Remove from heat. Let stand, covered, for 5 minutes. Fluff with a fork.

Broccoli-Chèvre Soufflé

Makes 4 servings

A soufflé is special anytime, but the distinctive tangy flavor of the chèvre (*shev*) cheese makes this soufflé extra-special.

Per Serving

Calories	304
Protein	14 g
Carbohydrate	12 g
Total Fat	22 g
Saturated Fat	8 g
Cholesterol	177 mg
Sodium	192 mg
Potassium	294 mg

¼ **cup chopped onion**
1 **clove garlic, minced**
3 **tablespoons olive oil *or* cooking oil**
¼ **cup all-purpose flour**
2 **tablespoons snipped fresh basil or 1 teaspoon dried basil, crushed**
¼ **teaspoon coarsely ground black pepper**

1 **cup milk**
1 **cup crumbled chèvre cheese (goat's cheese) (4 ounces)**
1 **cup finely chopped cooked broccoli**
  ▼
3 **egg yolks**
  ▼
3 **egg whites**

In a medium saucepan cook onion and garlic in olive oil or cooking oil till tender but not brown. Stir in flour, basil, and pepper. Add milk all at once. Cook and stir till thickened and bubbly. Remove from heat. Add crumbled cheese and stir till melted. Stir in broccoli.
▼ **In a medium mixing bowl** beat egg yolks with a fork till combined. Gradually add broccoli mixture, stirring constantly. Set aside.
▼ **In a medium mixing bowl** beat egg whites till stiff peaks form (tips stand straight). Gently fold about *1 cup* of the beaten egg whites into the broccoli mixture to lighten it. Gradually pour broccoli mixture over remaining beaten egg whites, folding to combine. Pour into a greased 1½-quart soufflé dish. ▼ **Bake** in a 350° oven about 40 minutes or till a knife inserted near the center comes out clean. Serve immediately.

BROCCOLI

Oriental Broccoli Stir-Fry

Makes 4 servings

This tasty side dish incorporates several oriental ingredients— rice vinegar, toasted sesame oil, and gingerroot. Look for the products at your supermarket, specialty food store, or oriental grocer.

1 **tablespoon soy sauce**
1 **tablespoon rice vinegar**
   or **white vinegar**
1 **teaspoon sugar**
½ **teaspoon grated gingerroot**
½ **teaspoon toasted sesame oil**

1 **clove garlic, minced**
   ▼
1 **tablespoon cooking oil**
3 **cups broccoli flowerets**
1 **small red *or* yellow sweet pepper, cut into ½-inch pieces (½ cup)**

Per Serving

Calories	64
Protein	2 g
Carbohydrate	6 g
Total Fat	4 g
Saturated Fat	1 g
Cholesterol	0 mg
Sodium	276 mg
Potassium	255 mg

For sauce, in a small mixing bowl stir together the soy sauce, rice vinegar, sugar, gingerroot, toasted sesame oil, and garlic. Set aside. ▼ **Pour the cooking oil** into a wok or large skillet. (Add more oil as necessary during cooking.) Preheat over medium-high heat. Add the broccoli; stir-fry for 2 minutes. Add the red or yellow sweet pepper; stir-fry for 1 to 2 minutes more or till vegetables are crisp-tender. Push vegetables from the center of the wok. Stir the sauce. Add the sauce to the center of the wok. Cook and stir till bubbly. Stir ingredients together to coat with sauce. Serve immediately.

BROCCOLI

Broccoli Purée with Crème Frâiche

Makes 4 servings

Spoon the left-over Crème Frâiche over fresh fruit for an easy dessert.

Per Serving

Calories	141
Protein	5 g
Carbohydrate	8 g
Total Fat	11 g
Saturated Fat	5 g
Cholesterol	26 mg
Sodium	196 mg
Potassium	341 mg

1 **pound broccoli**
▼
1/4 **cup Crème Frâiche**
2 **tablespoons dairy sour cream**
1 **tablepsoon margarine *or* butter, softened**
¼ **teaspoon pepper**
⅛ **teaspoon salt**

⅛ **teaspoon ground nutmeg**
▼
2 **tablespoons grated Parmesan *or* Romano cheese**
Julienne strips of oil-packed *or* rehydrated dried tomatoes

Wash broccoli; remove outer leaves and tough parts of broccoli stalks. Cut into ½-inch pieces. (You should have about 4 cups.) In a medium saucepan cook broccoli, covered, in a small amount of boiling salted water for 20 to 25 minutes or till very tender; drain. Cool slightly. ▼ **Transfer cooked broccoli** to a blender container or food processor bowl; add Crème Frâiche. Cover and blend or process till puréed, stopping to scrape down sides if necessary. Stir in sour cream, margarine or butter, pepper, salt, and nutmeg. ▼ **Pipe broccoli** mixture into 4 individual 6-ounce ramekins or casseroles. Sprinkle with Parmesan or Romano cheese. Bake, uncovered, in a 350° oven about 15 minutes or till heated through. Garnish with strips of dried tomatoes. Serve immediately.

Crème Frâiche

In a small saucepan heat ½ cup *whipping cream* over low heat till warm (90° to 100°). Pour the cream into a small bowl. Stir in 1 tablespoon *buttermilk*. Cover and let mixture stand at room temperature for 24 to 30 hours or till thickened. *Do not stir.* Store in a covered container in the refrigerator for up to a week. Stir before using. Makes ½ cup.

KOHLRABI

Sugar-Glazed Kohlrabi And Carrots

Makes 4 servings

Kohlrabi is
part of the
cabbage family,
but resembles
the turnip
in flavor and
texture.
Refrigerate
kohlrabi in a
plastic bag
for up to a
week.

1 tablespoon margarine *or* butter
3 small kohlrabies (about ¾ pound), peeled and cut into julienne strips (2¼ cups)

2 medium carrots, cut into julienne strips (1 cup)
▼
2 tablespoons margarine *or* butter
2 tablespoons brown sugar
¼ cup raisins

Per Serving

Calories	169
Protein	2 g
Carbohydrate	23 g
Total Fat	9 g
Saturated Fat	2 g
Cholesterol	0 mg
Sodium	143 mg
Potassium	455 mg

Place the 1 tablespoon margarine or butter in a wok or large skillet. (Add more margarine as necessary during cooking.) Preheat over medium-high heat. Add kohlrabi and carrots; stir-fry for 4 to 5 minutes or till vegetables are crisp-tender. Push vegetables from center of the wok.
▼**In the center of the wok** combine the 2 tablespoons margarine or butter and the brown sugar. Cook and stir about 30 seconds or till combined. Stir in raisins. Stir ingredients together to coat vegetables. Cook and stir about 2 minutes more or till heated through and the vegetables are glazed.

KOHLRABI

Kohlrabi and Pear Salad

Makes 4 servings.

Per Serving

Calories	211
Protein	3 g
Carbohydrate	20 g
Total Fat	15 g
Saturated Fat	2 g
Cholesterol	0 mg
Sodium	23 mg
Potassium	504 mg

4 **small kohlrabies (about 1 pound), peeled and cut into julienne strips (3 cups)**
1 **medium pear, cored and thinly sliced (1 cup)**
▼
3 **tablespoons salad oil**
3 **tablespoons white wine vinegar**

1 **tablespoon snipped fresh chives**
1 **tablespoon honey**
¼ **teaspoon pepper**
⅛ **teaspoon ground nutmeg**
▼
Red-tipped leaf lettuce
¼ **cup chopped pecans, toasted**

If available, choose a red pear, like red Bartlett, for this salad.

Cook kohlrabi, covered, in a small amount of boiling salted water for 6 to 8 minutes or till crisp-tender. Drain well. In a medium mixing bowl combine cooked kohlrabi and pear slices. ▼ **Meanwhile,** for marinade, in a screw-top jar combine salad oil, white wine vinegar, chives, honey, pepper, and nutmeg. Cover and shake well. Pour marinade over kohlrabi and pear slices. Toss lightly to coat. Cover and chill for 4 to 24 hours, stirring occasionally. ▼ **To serve,** line 4 salad plates with lettuce leaves. Divide kohlrabi and pear slices evenly among the lettuce-lined plates. Sprinkle each serving with pecans.

KOHLRABI

Kohlrabi Parmesan

Makes 4 servings

3 **tablespoons margarine** *or* **butter**

4 **small kohlrabies (about 1 pound), peeled and coarsely shredded (3 cups)**

1 **medium red** *or* **green sweet pepper, chopped (¾ cup)**

1 **medium carrot, coarsely shredded (½ cup)**

¼ **cup grated Parmesan** *or* **Romano cheese**

2 **teaspoons snipped fresh thyme** *or* **½ teaspoon dried thyme, crushed**

⅛ **teaspoon salt**

⅛ **teaspoon cracked black pepper**

Grated Parmesan *or* **Romano cheese (optional)**

Fresh thyme

Kohlrabi is usually pale green on the outside, although purple varieties may be found. Both varieties have white flesh.

In a large skillet melt margarine or butter. Stir in shredded kohlrabi, chopped red or green sweet pepper, and shredded carrot. Cook and stir for 4 to 5 minutes or till vegetables are crisp-tender. Stir in Parmesan or Romano cheese, thyme, salt, and pepper. Sprinkle with additional Parmesan or Romano cheese, if desired. Garnish with fresh thyme.

CUCUMBER

Cucumber Smoked Salmon Bites

Makes 16 appetizer sandwiches

You can make these fancy appetizers up to 1 hour before serving.

¾ **cup soft-style cream cheese**

¼ **cup finely chopped cucumber**

1 **tablespoon snipped fresh dill** *or* **1 teaspoon dried dillweed**

Milk

1 **2-ounce piece smoked salmon with skin and bones removed, flaked**

▼

16 **slices rye** *or* **pumpernickel bread** *or* **party bread slices**

⅓ **of a small cucumber**

▼

Fresh dill

Per Serving

Calories	70
Protein	2 g
Carbohydrate	6 g
Total Fat	4 g
Saturated Fat	2 g
Cholesterol	12 mg
Sodium	124 mg
Potassium	78 mg

In a small mixing bowl stir the cream cheese till softened. Stir in the ¼ cup finely chopped cucumber and the 1 tablespoon dill. Add milk, if necessary, to make of spreading consistency. Gently fold in the salmon; *do not overmix.* Set aside. ▼ **Cut each bread slice** into a 3-inch circle or square, removing the crusts (not necessary if using party bread). Set bread aside. Score the peel of the small cucumber with the tines of a fork; cut into 16 thin slices. With a sharp knife, make a cut from the outside edge to the center of each slice of cucumber. Twist the ends in opposite directions to form a twist. Set aside. ▼ **To serve,** spread about *1 tablespoon* of the salmon mixture on each slice of bread. Top each with a cucumber twist and garnish with fresh dill.

CUCUMBERS

Cucumbers Oriental

Makes 4 to 6 servings

An oriental version of marinated cucumbers.

Per Serving

Calories	29
Protein	1 g
Carbohydrate	4 g
Total Fat	1 g
Saturated Fat	0 g
Cholesterol	0 mg
Sodium	88 mg
Potassium	160 mg

2 **medium cucumbers**
▼
2 **tablespoons rice vinegar**
1 **to 2 jalapeño peppers, seeded and finely chopped (1 to 2 tablespoons)**

1 **tablespoon soy sauce**
1 **tablespoon salad oil**
2 **teaspoons sugar**
½ **teaspoon toasted sesame oil**
½ **teaspoon grated gingerroot**

Halve cucumbers lengthwise; seed and thinly slice. Set aside. ▼ **In a screw-top** jar combine rice vinegar, chopped jalapeño pepper, soy sauce, salad oil, sugar, sesame oil, and gingerroot. Cover and shake well. Pour over cucumbers. Toss lightly to mix. Cover and chill for 2 to 24 hours. Serve with a slotted spoon.

CUCUMBER

Cucumber Salad

Makes 4 to 6 servings

You can keep cucumbers in your refrigerator for up to 2 weeks.

2 medium cucumbers, thinly sliced (3½ cups)
1 small yellow sweet pepper, cut into julienne strips (¾ cup)
▼
2 tablespoons walnut oil *or* salad oil
1 tablespoon water
1 tablespoon red wine vinegar

1 tablespoon snipped fresh basil *or* ½ teaspoon dried basil, crushed
⅛ teaspoon salt
⅛ teaspoon pepper
Dash ground red pepper
▼
3 tablespoons chopped walnuts, toasted

Per Serving

Calories	117
Protein	2 g
Carbohydrate	6 g
Total Fat	10 g
Saturated Fat	1 g
Cholesterol	0 mg
Sodium	136 mg
Potassium	229 mg

In a medium mixing bowl combine cucumber slices and sweet pepper strips. Set aside. ▼ **For vinaigrette,** in a screw-top jar combine walnut oil or salad oil, water, red wine vinegar, basil, salt, pepper, and dash ground red pepper. Cover and shake well. Pour vinaigrette over cucumber mixture. Toss lightly to coat. Cover and refrigerate for 4 to 24 hours. ▼ **Before serving,** stir in walnuts.

VEGGIE COMBO

Best-of-the-Garden Platter

Makes about 12 appetizer servings

Per Serving

Calories	81
Protein	3 g
Carbohydrate	17g
Total Fat	1 g
Saturated Fat	0 g
Cholesterol	2 mg
Sodium	43 mg
Potassium	457 mg

8 to 12 tiny whole carrots
16 to 24 green beans,
   trimmed
6 small yellow summer
   squash, cut into 1-inch
   pieces
   ▼
3 or 4 large sweet peppers
   (yellow, purple, red,
   and/or green)

1 cup yellow or red
   cherry tomatoes
1 medium cucumber
   Fresh herbs (optional)
   Edible flowers (optional)
   Creamy Salsa Dip
   Chutney Dip
   Lemon-Dill Dip

Forget the usual celery sticks and purchased sour cream dip! This updated vegetable and dip platter uses an interesting variety of summer produce plus three creamy, low-fat dips.

To trim carrots, leave 1 to 2 inches of stem, if you like; do not peel. In a saucepan combine carrots, beans, squash, and a small amount of water. Bring to boiling; reduce heat. Simmer, covered, for 5 minutes; drain and cool. Cover and chill till serving time. ▼ **At serving time,** remove tops and seeds from sweet peppers; cut into rings or strips. Halve any large cherry tomatoes. Cut cucumber into strips or slices. On a large platter arrange cooked vegetables, peppers, tomatoes, and cucumber. Garnish with fresh herbs and edible flowers, if desired. Serve with assorted dips.

Creamy Salsa Dip

Combine ½ cup plain yogurt, ½ cup *salsa,* and ⅓ cup *reduced-calorie mayonnaise or salad dressing.* Cover and chill till serving time. Makes about 1¼ cups.

Chutney Dip

Combine one 8-ounce carton *plain yogurt;* 3 tablespoons snipped *chutney;* 1 *green onion,* chopped (2 tablespoons); and 1 teaspoon *curry powder.* Cover and chill till serving time. Makes about 1 cup.

Lemon-Dill Dip

Combine ½ cup *low-fat dairy sour cream;* 3 ounces *cream cheese or Neufchâtel cheese,* softened; 1 tablespoon snipped *fresh dill or* 1 teaspoon *dried dillweed;* 1 teaspoon *lemon juice;* 2 cloves *garlic,* minced; ¼ teaspoon *onion powder;* and ⅛ teaspoon *salt.* Cover and chill till serving time. Stir in enough *milk* (1 to 2 tablespoons) to make of dipping consistency. Makes about ¾ cup.

VEGGIE COMBO

Garden Vegetable Pasta Toss

Makes 6 servings

What a summertime extravaganza! This recipe combines squash, leeks, carrots, green beans, and fresh herbs all into one luscious side dish.

4 ounces fusilli, fettuccine, *or* linguine, broken in half
⅓ cup dry white wine
¼ teaspoon salt
Nonstick spray coating
3 medium carrots, cut into julienne strips (1½ cups)
1½ cups green beans bias sliced into 2-inch pieces
2 medium leeks (8 ounces), cut into ½-inch-thick slices (⅔ cup)
1 tablespoon snipped fresh basil *or* ½ teaspoon dried basil, crushed
1 tablespoon snipped fresh dill *or* ½ teaspoon dried dillweed

1 clove garlic, minced
▼
1 medium yellow summer squash, cut into julienne strips (1½ cups)
1 fresh red cayenne chili pepper, seeded and finely chopped (½ teaspoon), *or* ⅛ teaspoon ground red pepper
2 tablespoons water
½ cup finely shredded asiago *or* Parmesan cheese
Fresh red cayenne chili peppers (optional)

Per Serving

Calories	170
Protein	8 g
Carbohydrate	27 g
Total Fat	3 g
Saturated Fat	0 g
Cholesterol	7 mg
Sodium	226 mg
Potassium	323 mg

Cook pasta according to package directions. Meanwhile, combine wine, salt, and ground red pepper (if using); set aside. Spray a wok with nonstick spray coating. Preheat wok over medium heat. Add carrots, beans, leeks, basil, dill, and garlic. Stir-fry for 3 minutes. ▼ **Add squash,** fresh red pepper (if using), and water. Cover wok and cook for 5 to 6 minutes more or till vegetables are crisp-tender. Drain pasta; add to vegetables. Drizzle with wine mixture. Toss gently. Transfer to a serving platter. Sprinkle with asiago or Parmesan cheese. Garnish with additional fresh red pepper, if desired.

VEGGIE COMBO

Corn and Cucumber Relish

Makes 2 cups (sixteen 2-tablespoon servings)

Here's an out-of-the-ordinary relish with oriental over-tones from gingerroot, toasted sesame oil, and red pepper.

1 **medium cucumber, seeded and chopped (1¼ cups)**
2 **teaspoons salt**
▼
1 **cup fresh cut corn**
½ **cup sugar**
½ **cup white wine vinegar**
2 **green onions, thinly sliced (¼ cup)**

1 **teaspoon grated gingerroot**
▼
2 **tablespoons diced pimiento**
½ **teaspoon toasted sesame oil**
⅛ **teaspoon ground red pepper**

Per Serving

Calories	27
Protein	1 g
Carbohydrate	7 g
Total Fat	0 g
Saturated Fat	0 g
Cholesterol	0 mg
Sodium	136 mg
Potassium	64 mg

In a medium mixing bowl sprinkle the chopped cucumber with salt. Let stand for 20 minutes. Rinse the cucumber; drain well, pressing out the excess liquid. ▼ **Meanwhile,** in a medium saucepan combine corn, sugar, vinegar, green onion, and gingerroot. Bring to boiling, stirring occasionally. Reduce heat; simmer, uncovered, for 4 minutes. Remove from heat. ▼ **Stir in** the drained cucumber, diced pimiento, toasted sesame oil, and red pepper. Transfer mixture to a nonmetallic container. Refrigerate, covered, at least 8 hours before serving. Refrigerate any leftovers, covered, for up to 1 week. Drain mixture before serving.

VEGGIE COMBO

Garden Vegetables with Horseradish Sauce

Makes 4 to 5 servings

Per Serving

Calories	296
Protein	4 g
Carbohydrate	16 g
Total Fat	25 g
Saturated Fat	4 g
Cholesterol	16 mg
Sodium	406 mg
Potassium	413 mg

1½ cups cauliflower flowerets
3 medium carrots, sliced
   ½ inch thick (1½ cups)
½ pound broccoli, cut into
   1-inch pieces (1¾ cups)
▼
½ cup mayonnaise *or* salad
   dressing
2 tablespoons finely
   chopped onion

4 teaspoons prepared
   horseradish
⅛ teaspoon salt
   Dash pepper
▼
¼ cup fine dry bread
   crumbs
1 tablespoon margarine *or*
   butter, melted
   Dash paprika

A perfect match for grilled steaks, this tasty fresh veggie dish gets its tang from horseradish.

In a 2-quart saucepan cook cauliflower and carrots, covered, in a small amount of boiling water for 5 minutes. Add broccoli and cook 5 minutes more or till vegetables are crisp-tender. Drain. ▼ **Meanwhile,** in a small mixing bowl combine mayonnaise or salad dressing, onion, horseradish, salt, and pepper. In a 1½-quart casserole combine cooked vegetables and mayonnaise mixture. ▼ **In a small mixing bowl** combine bread crumbs, margarine or butter, and paprika; sprinkle over vegetable mixture. ▼ **Bake,** uncovered, in a 350° oven for 15 minutes or till heated through and topping is golden.

VEGGIE COMBO

Easy Vegetable Casserole

Makes 4 to 5 servings

This spoon-bread-style dish is a delicious way to use up little dabs of garden vegetables.

¾ cup cut fresh corn
¼ cup chopped onion
¼ cup chopped green
  pepper
¼ cup water
▼
½ cup chopped yellow
  summer squash *or*
  zucchini
1 small tomato, chopped
  (½ cup)

½ cup shredded cheddar
  cheese (2 ounces)
⅓ cup cornmeal
⅓ cup milk
1 slightly beaten egg
½ teaspoon salt
¼ teaspoon pepper
  Few dashes bottled hot
  pepper sauce
▼
2 tablespoons shredded
  cheddar cheese

Per Serving

Calories	181
Protein	9 g
Carbohydrate	20 g
Total Fat	8 g
Saturated Fat	4 g
Cholesterol	73 mg
Sodium	409 mg
Potassium	259 mg

In a medium saucepan combine corn, onion, green pepper, and water. Bring to boiling; reduce heat. Cover and simmer for 5 minutes or till vegetables are crisp-tender. *Do not drain.* ▼ **Meanwhile,** in large mixing bowl combine chopped yellow summer squash or zucchini, chopped tomato, the ½ cup cheese, cornmeal, milk, egg, salt, pepper, and hot pepper sauce. Add *undrained* vegetables to cornmeal mixture; mix well. Transfer to a greased 1-quart casserole. ▼ **Bake,** uncovered, in a 350° oven for 35 to 40 minutes or till a knife inserted near the center comes out clean. Top with the 2 tablespoons cheese.

VEGGIE COMBO

Grilled Summer Vegetable Potpourri

Makes 4 to 6 servings

This is a great totable food for your away-from-home picnic. Just bundle up everything in the foil and tote it to your picnic site.

Per Serving

Calories	81
Protein	2 g
Carbohydrate	11 g
Total Fat	4 g
Saturated Fat	1 g
Cholesterol	0 mg
Sodium	110 mg
Potassium	415 mg

1 tablespoon cooking oil
1 tablespoon white wine vinegar
1 tablespoon white wine Worcestershire sauce
1 teaspoon snipped fresh tarragon *or* ¼ teaspoon dried tarragon, crushed
½ teaspoon finely shredded lemon peel
⅛ teaspoon salt
▼
2 small yellow summer squash, halved length-wise and cut into ½-inch-thick slices (about 2 cups)

8 ounces large whole mushrooms, halved (about 12)
1 cup pearl onions *or* 1 large onion, cut into chunks
1 large stalk celery, bias-sliced into 1-inch pieces
2 tablespoons sliced pimiento

Tear off a 36x18-inch piece of heavy-duty foil. Fold in half to make an 18-inch square. Fold up sides, using your fist to form a pouch. ▼ **In a small mixing bowl** stir together the cooking oil, white wine vinegar, white wine Worcestershire sauce, tarragon, lemon peel, and salt. ▼ **In the foil pouch** combine the summer squash, mushrooms, onions, celery, and pimiento. Pour oil mixture over the vegetables. Fold edges of foil to seal pouch securely, leaving space for expansion of steam. ▼ **Grill on an** uncovered grill directly over *medium-hot* coals about 30 minutes or till the vegetables are crisp-tender, turning the pouch occasionally.

VEGGIE COMBO

Green and Gold Stir-Fry

Makes 4 servings

The scalloped sunburst squash adds a novel shape and buttery flavor to this stir-fry.

Nonstick spray coating
3 medium leeks, thinly sliced (1 cup)
1 tablespoon snipped fresh oregano *or* ¼ teaspoon dried oregano, crushed
1 clove garlic, minced
▼
1 to 2 tablespoons olive oil *or* cooking oil
½ teaspoon toasted sesame oil

2 cups broccoli flowerets
2 cups yellow sunburst squash *or* yellow summer squash, cut into small wedges
Lemon wedges
Fresh basil (optional)

Per Serving

Calories	115
Protein	4 g
Carbohydrate	18 g
Total Fat	5 g
Saturated Fat	1 g
Cholesterol	0 mg
Sodium	33 mg
Potassium	475 mg

Spray a wok or large skillet with nonstick coating. Preheat over medium heat. Add leeks, oregano, and garlic; stir-fry for 2 to 3 minutes or till leeks are tender. Remove from wok or skillet; set aside.
▼ **Add** 1 tablespoon olive oil or cooking oil and the toasted sesame oil to wok. Add broccoil and squash; stir-fry for 3 to 4 minutes or till vegetables are crisp-tender, adding remaining oil if necessary. Return leek mixture to wok; heat through. Serve with lemon wedges. Garnish with additional basil, if desired.

VEGGIE COMBO

Pasta Primavera

Makes 4 servings

If you want to use one of the refrigerated pastas that are in the supermarket, increase the amount of pasta to 6 ounces.

3 ounces packaged spinach fettuccine *or* linguine
1 small zucchini *or* yellow summer squash, halved lengthwise and sliced (1 cup)
1 cup pea pods, tips and strings removed, halved lengthwise
1 small yellow *or* red sweet pepper, chopped (½ cup)
  ▼
2 large tomatoes, peeled and coarsely chopped (2½ cups)

2 green onions, thinly sliced (¼ cup)
2 tablespoons snipped fresh basil *or* dill *or* 1 teaspoon dried basil *or* dillweed, crushed
1 tablespoon olive oil *or* cooking oil
2 tablespoons grated Parmesan cheese
  Coarsely cracked black pepper

Per Serving

Calories	154
Protein	6 g
Carbohydrate	22 g
Total Fat	5 g
Saturated Fat	1 g
Cholesterol	2 mg
Sodium	74 mg
Potassium	330 mg

Cook pasta according to package directions. Add zucchini or yellow summer squash, pea pods, and yellow or red sweet pepper to pasta in boiling water for last 3 minutes of cooking. Vegetables should be crisp-tender. Drain. ▼ **In a medium saucepan** heat the tomatoes, green onion, and basil or dill in hot oil for 2 to 3 minutes or till heated through, stirring gently. ▼ **Toss the pasta** mixture with the tomato mixture. Transfer to a warm serving platter. Sprinkle with Parmesan cheese and pepper.

Summer Vegetable Casserole

Makes 5 to 6 servings

Green beans, summer squash, tomatoes, and pasta in a Swiss cheese sauce tag this down-home casserole a winner.

Per Serving

Calories	209
Protein	9 g
Carbohydrate	30 g
Total Fat	6 g
Saturated Fat	3 g
Cholesterol	10 mg
Sodium	359 mg
Potassium	514 mg

1½ cups green beans bias-sliced into 2-inch pieces
1¼ cups medium bow-tie pasta (about 3 ounces)
1 medium yellow summer squash, cut into julienne strips (1½ cups)
▼
1 cup sliced mushrooms
1 medium onion, chopped (½ cup)
4 teaspoons snipped fresh basil *or* ¾ teaspoon dried basil, crushed
1 tablespoon snipped fresh oregano *or* 1 teaspoon dried oregano, crushed
1 tablespoon margarine *or* butter

1 tablespoon all-purpose flour
¼ teaspoon salt
⅛ teaspoon pepper
1 cup milk
¼ cup shredded process Swiss cheese (1 ounce)
2 to 3 teaspoons Dijon-style mustard
Few drops bottled hot pepper sauce
▼
2 *or* 3 plum tomatoes, diagonally sliced (about 1 cup)
▼
½ cup soft bread crumbs
2 tablespoons grated Parmesan cheese

In a saucepan cook green beans, covered, in 4 cups salted boiling water for 5 minutes. Add pasta. Return to boiling; boil 5 minutes more. Add squash; return to boiling and boil gently 5 minutes more or till vegetables and pasta are tender. Drain. Set aside. ▼ **Meanwhile,** for cheese sauce, cook mushrooms, onion, basil, and oregano in hot margarine till tender. Stir in flour, salt, and pepper. Add milk all at once. Cook and stir till bubbly. Stir in Swiss cheese, mustard, and hot pepper sauce; cook 1 minute more. ▼ **Gently toss** cheese sauce with pasta-vegetable mixture. Add tomatoes; toss gently. Spoon mixture into a 1½-quart casserole. ▼ **For topping,** mix bread crumbs and Parmesan cheese. (You may cover and chill casserole and crumb mixture separately at this point for up to 2 days.) Sprinkle topping over casserole. Bake in a 400° oven 20 to 25 minutes or till hot (35 minutes, if chilled).

ASIAN PRODUCE

As the popularity of oriental cooking continues to grow, expect to see more Amerasian foods like bitter melon, daikon, and cilantro at farmer's markets. These tips will help you become familiar with the makings for Asian Gazpacho (see recipe, opposite).

Bitter melon: Not melon at all, this fruit, which resembles a cucumber with bumpy skin, is really a squash. About 6 inches long, bitter melon has a cucumber texture with small seeds and a sour-bland squash flavor. Refrigerate bitter melon, tightly wrapped, for up to 2 days. (Bitter melon becomes soft when stored next to tomatoes, bananas, or avocados from the gases they give off.) To use, halve lengthwise and scrape out the seeds with a spoon. Enjoy the meaty, bitter-tasting squash raw or cooked as you would zucchini.

Daikon (*DIE kuhn*): This white, carrot-shaped, Japanese radish ranges from 6 to 15 inches in length with an average diameter of 2 to 3 inches. The daikon's flesh is juicy and white with a mildly spicy, radishlike flavor. Look for firm daikons with smooth, white skin. Refrigerate daikons in a plastic bag for up to 2 weeks. To use, peel off the outer layer as you would a carrot. Chop, slice, or shred to enjoy raw or stir-fried.

Cilantro: These small, fragile, green leaves from the coriander plant are also known as Chinese parsley. Cilantro has a pungent, almost musty odor and taste that gives a distinctive flavor to oriental dishes, as well as to Mexican and other Latin American cuisines. Use it sparingly when you first try it. Rinse and snip, as for other herbs, before using. Store it in a plastic bag in the refrigerator.

Asian Gazpacho shown with bitter melon

Asian Gazpacho

Makes 6 to 8 servings

4 ounces bitter melon *or* 1 small zucchini

▼

4 cups chicken broth
1 large red or green sweet pepper, chopped (1⅓ cups)
1 medium cucumber, chopped (1 cup)
4 green onions, thinly sliced (½ cup)
1 stalk celery, chopped (½ cup)
½ cup chopped daikon (Japanese radish)

⅓ cup rice vinegar *or* white wine vinegar
¼ cup snipped fresh cilantro (optional)
1 tablespoon soy sauce
1½ teaspoons toasted sesame oil
Few dashes bottled hot pepper sauce

▼

½ cup enoki mushrooms (optional)

Serve bowls of this chilled soup, which shows off several Asian vegetables, as an appetizer, or as a light meal along with a sandwich or salad.

Halve bitter melon lengthwise; remove seeds. Cut bitter melon or zucchini into julienne strips. (You should have about 1 cup). ▼ **In a large bowl** combine bitter melon or zucchini, broth, sweet pepper, cucumber, green onion, celery, daikon, rice vinegar, cilantro (if desired), soy sauce, toasted sesame oil, and hot pepper sauce. Cover and chill for 4 hours or overnight. ▼ **To serve,** ladle into soup bowls. Top with enoki mushrooms, if desired.

APRICOTS

Jumbo Apricot-Bran Muffins

Makes 6 large or 15 small muffins

Dive into one of these giant muffins flavored with buttermilk, cinnamon, and nutmeg while they're still warm.

1½ cups all-purpose flour
1 cup whole bran cereal
1 teaspoon baking soda
1 teaspoon ground cinnamon
¼ teaspoon salt
¼ teaspoon ground nutmeg

▼
1 beaten egg
1 cup buttermilk
½ cup packed brown sugar
¼ cup cooking oil
¾ cup finely chopped apricots (1 to 2)

Per Serving

Calories	331
Protein	8 g
Carbohydrate	55 g
Total Fat	11 g
Saturated Fat	2 g
Cholesterol	37 mg
Sodium	446 mg
Potassium	413 mg

Grease six 4-inch muffin cups or six 6-ounce custard cups or line with large paper bake cups. Set muffin cups aside. ▼ **In a large mixing bowl** stir together flour, whole bran cereal, baking soda, cinnamon, salt, and nutmeg. Make a well in the center of the dry ingredients.
▼ **In a medium mixing bowl** combine egg, buttermilk, brown sugar, and oil. Add egg mixture all at once to dry ingredients. Stir *just till moistened* (batter should be lumpy). Carefully fold in chopped apricots.
▼ **Spoon batter** into the prepared muffins cups or custard cups, filling each ¾ full. Bake in a 375° oven for 25 to 30 minutes or till a toothpick inserted near the center of a muffin comes out clean. Remove muffins from muffin cups or custard cups and cool slightly on a wire rack. Serve warm.
Note: To make smaller muffins, grease fifteen 2½-inch muffin cups or line with paper bake cups. Fill each ⅔ full with batter. Bake in a 400° oven for 15 to 20 minutes or till toothpick comes out clean.

APRICOTS

Apricot-Filled Jelly Roll

Makes 10 servings

Per Serving

Calories	307
Protein	4 g
Carbohydrate	52 g
Total Fat	10 g
Saturated Fat	3 g
Cholesterol	95 mg
Sodium	138 mg
Potassium	182 mg

½ **cup all-purpose flour**
1 **teaspoon baking powder**
1 **teaspoon ground cinnamon**
¼ **teaspoon ground nutmeg**
¼ **teaspoon ground cloves**
¼ **teaspoon ground ginger**
▼
4 **egg yolks**
⅓ **cup sugar**

▼
4 **egg whites**
½ **cup sugar**
▼
1 **pound apricots (8 to 12), chopped (2 cups)**
⅓ **cup water**
3 **tablespoons sugar**
4 **teaspoons cornstarch**
▼
Cream Cheese Frosting

Dress up the top of this cake with an easy yet elegant, idea. Place a small paper doily or craft stencil over the frosting. Lightly sift ground cinnamon over the doily. Remove the doily carefully.

Grease and flour a 15x10x1-inch jelly-roll pan. Set aside. Mix flour, baking powder, cinnamon, nutmeg, cloves, and ginger. Set aside. ▼ **Beat egg yolks** with a mixer on high speed 5 minutes or till thick. Gradually add ⅓ cup sugar, beating on high speed till sugar is almost dissolved. Wash beaters. ▼ **Beat egg whites** on medium to high speed till soft peaks form (tips curl). Gradually add ½ cup sugar, about *2 tablespoons* at a time, beating on medium to high speed till stiff peaks form (tips stand straight). Fold about *1 cup* of the egg white mixture into yolk mixture. Fold yolk mixture into remaining egg white mixture. Fold in flour mixture. Spread in pan. ▼ **Bake** in a 375° oven 12 to 15 minutes or till cake springs back when touched. Immediately loosen cake from pan. Invert onto a towel sprinkled with powdered sugar. Roll up cake and towel, jelly-roll style, starting from one of the short sides. Cool.
▼ **Meanwhile,** for filling, bring apricots and water to boiling; reduce heat. Cover; simmer 5 minutes. Mix 3 tablespoons sugar and cornstarch. Stir into apricot mixture. Cook and stir till bubbly. Cook and stir 2 minutes more. Cover surface with plastic wrap. Set aside to cool. *Do not stir.* ▼ **Unroll cake.** Spread filling over cake to within ½ inch of edges. Roll up cake as before without towel. Frost with Cream Cheese Frosting. If desired, garnish with additional apricots. Store in refrigerator.

Cream Cheese Frosting

Beat together one 3-ounce package *cream cheese;* ¼ cup *margarine or butter,* softened; and 1 teaspoon *vanilla.* Gradually add 2 cups sifted *powdered sugar* and beat to make a spreading consistency.

APRICOTS

Apricot and Ham Pasta Salad

Makes 4 main-dish servings

Look for apricots in your supermarket from late May through mid-August. Be sure to choose plump, firm fruit with a red blush and avoid fruit that is pale yellow or green-yellow.

1⅓ cups cavatelli (4 ounces)
▼
1 pound apricots (8 to 12), pitted and sliced (2 cups)
½ pound lean cooked ham *or* pork, cut into thin strips (1½ cups)
1 small zucchini, halved lengthwise and sliced (1 cup)

1 medium red sweet pepper, cut into julienne strips (1 cup)
½ cup cubed creamy Havarti cheese (2 ounces)
▼
Apricot Dressing
▼
Curly Endive *or* lettuce leaves

Per Serving

Calories	419
Protein	20 g
Carbohydrate	35 g
Total Fat	23 g
Saturated Fat	3 g
Cholesterol	34 mg
Sodium	985 mg
Potassium	549 mg

Cook pasta according to package directions. Drain pasta. Rinse with cold water; drain again. ▼ **In a large mixing bowl** combine pasta, apricot slices, ham or pork strips, zucchini, red pepper strips, and cheese. ▼ **Pour** ⅔ *cup* of the Apricot Dressing over pasta mixture. Toss lightly to coat. Cover and chill salad and remaining dressing for 4 to 24 hours. ▼ **To serve,** line 4 salad plates with curly endive or lettuce leaves. Divide pasta mixture evenly among plates. Pass remaining dressing.

Apricot Dressing

In a blender container or food processor bowl combine 2 *apricots,* pitted and quartered; 3 tablespoons *white wine vinegar;* 1 tablespoon *sugar;* ½ teaspoon *salt;* and ⅛ teaspoon *pepper.* Cover and blend or process till smooth. With blender or food processor running, add ¼ cup *salad oil* in a thin, steady stream. Continue blending for 2 to 3 minutes or till thick. Stir in 1 tablespoon snipped *fresh basil or* 1 teaspoon *dried basil,* crushed. Makes about 1 cup.

PEACHES

Peach Clafouti
With Citrus Sauce

Makes 4 servings

2 medium peaches, peeled, pitted, and sliced (2 cups)
2 tablespoons sugar
2 cups evaporated milk
3 eggs
¼ cup all-purpose flour

3 tablespoons sugar
½ teaspoon almond extract
½ teaspoon vanilla
Dash salt

▼

Citrus Sauce

Clafouti is a rich, country-French dessert that's made by topping a layer of fresh fruit with batter. It's easy to make and delicious to eat.

In an 8x1½-inch round baking dish combine peaches and the 2 tablespoons sugar. In a blender container combine evaporated milk, eggs, flour, the 3 tablespoons sugar, almond extract, vanilla, and salt. Cover and blend for 15 seconds. Pour over fruit. ▼ **Bake** in a 375° oven for 40 to 45 minutes or till a knife inserted in custard near center comes out clean. Serve warm with Citrus Sauce.

Citrus Sauce

In a saucepan combine ⅓ cup *sugar* and 2 teaspoons *cornstarch*. Stir in ⅔ cup *water*. Cook and stir over medium heat till thickened and bubbly. Cook and stir for 2 minutes more. Remove from heat. Stir in 2 tablespoons *orange juice* and 1 tablespoon *lemon juice*. Makes about 1 cup.

Fruited Chicken

Makes 4 main-dish servings

Serve this scrumptious braised chicken dish, loaded with peaches, pecans, and basil, on a bed of wild rice.

2 **pounds meaty chicken pieces (breasts, thighs, and drumsticks)**
2 **tablespoons cooking oil**
1 **cup chicken broth**
¼ **cup peach nectar**
1 **tablespoon snipped parsley**
1 **tablespoon snipped fresh basil** *or* **½ teaspoon dried basil, crushed**

¼ **teaspoon salt**
2 **medium peaches, peeled, pitted, and sliced (2 cups)**

▼

2 **tablespoons chicken broth** *or* **peach nectar**
4 **teaspoons cornstarch**
¼ **cup chopped pecans**
2 **cups hot cooked wild rice**

Per Serving

Calories	506
Protein	39 g
Carbohydrate	33 g
Total Fat	24 g
Saturated Fat	5 g
Cholesterol	104 mg
Sodium	448 mg
Potassium	627 mg

Skin chicken, if desired. Rinse and pat dry. In a large skillet cook chicken pieces in hot cooking oil about 10 minutes or till lightly browned, turning to brown evenly. Drain fat. Add the 1 cup chicken broth, peach nectar, parsley, basil and salt. Bring to boiling; reduce heat. Cover and simmer for 15 minutes. Add sliced peaches. Cover and simmer for 10 to 15 minutes or till chicken is tender and no longer pink.

▼ **Transfer chicken** and peaches to a serving platter. Cover and keep warm. For sauce, in a small mixing bowl stir together the 2 tablespoons chicken broth and cornstarch. Stir into broth mixture in the skillet. Cook and stir till thickened and bubbly. Cook and stir for 2 minute more. Pour some sauce over chicken and peaches. Sprinkle with chopped pecans. Pass remaining sauce. Serve with wild rice.

Peach Dumplings with Brandy Sauce

Makes 4 servings

Per Serving

Calories	992
Protein	10 g
Carbohydrate	110 g
Total Fat	58 g
Saturated Fat	19 g
Cholesterol	114 mg
Sodium	547 mg
Potassium	398 mg

1½ **cups water**
¾ **cup sugar**
¼ **teaspoon ground cinnamon**
¼ **teaspoon ground nutmeg**
2 **tablespoons margarine** *or* **butter**
▼
2 **cups all-purpose flour**
½ **teaspoon salt**
⅓ **cup margarine** *or* **butter**

⅓ **cup shortening**
6 **to 7 tablespoons cold water**
▼
4 **medium peaches, peeled, halved, and pitted**
2 **tablespoons raisins**
2 **tablespoons finely chopped nuts**
▼
Brandy Sauce

For syrup, in a medium saucepan combine the 1½ cups water, sugar, cinnamon, and nutmeg. Bring to boiling. Reduce heat and simmer for 5 minutes. Remove from heat; stir in the 2 tablespoons margarine or butter. ▼ **For pastry,** in a medium mixing bowl stir together the flour and salt. Using a pastry blender, cut in the ⅓ cup margarine or butter and the shortening till pieces are the size of small peas. Sprinkle *1 tablespoon* of the 6 to 7 tablespoons cold water over part of the flour mixture; gently toss with a fork. Push moistened dough to the side of the bowl. Repeat till all dough is moistened. Form dough into a ball. ▼ **On a lightly floured surface,** flatten dough with your hands. Roll dough into a 14-inch square. Cut pastry into four 7-inch squares. Place *one* peach half, cut side up, on center of each pastry square. Combine raisins and nuts; spoon mixture into centers of fruit. Place remaining fruit halves on top of filled fruit. ▼ **Moisten edges of pastry** with water. Fold corners to the center on top of the fruit, pinching edges together to seal. Place dumplings in an 8x8x2-inch baking dish. Pour syrup over dumplings. ▼ **Bake** in a 375° oven about 45 minutes or till golden. Serve warm with Brandy Sauce.

Brandy Cream

In a small saucepan cook and stir 1 beaten *egg*, ¾ cup *whipping cream*, and ¼ *sugar* over medium heat till thickened and just bubbly. Remove from heat; stir in 1 tablespoon *brandy*. Serve warm. Makes about 1 cup.

PEACHES

Peach-Raspberry Cobbler
Makes 6 servings

1 **cup all-purpose flour**
¼ **cup sugar**
1 **teaspoon baking powder**
½ **teaspoon ground cinnamon**
3 **tablespoons margarine *or* butter**
1 **beaten egg**
3 **tablespoons milk**
▼
½ **cup sugar**
1 **tablespoon cornstarch**
2 **tablespoons water**

4 **medium peaches, peeled, pitted, and sliced (4 cups)**
1 **teaspoon finely shredded lemon peel**
1 **teaspoon lemon juice**
2 **cups raspberries**
▼
1 **teaspoon sugar**
▼
Ice cream *or* sweetened whipped cream

For a delicious alternative, substitute 4 cups sliced unpeeled nectarines for the peaches, and use 2 cups sliced plums for the raspberries. Add the plums at the same time as the nectarines to the cornstarch mixture.

For biscuit topping, in a medium mixing bowl stir together the flour, the ¼ cup sugar, baking powder, and cinnamon. Cut in margarine or butter till mixture resembles coarse crumbs. Combine egg and milk; set aside. ▼ **For filling,** in a medium saucepan combine the ½ cup sugar and cornstarch; add water. Stir in peach slices, lemon peel, and lemon juice. Cook and stir till thickened and bubbly. Gently fold in raspberries. Return just to boiling, stirring gently to avoid breaking up the fruit. Transfer hot filling to a shallow 2-quart casserole. ▼ **Add the egg** mixture all at once to the dry ingredients, stirring just till moistened. Immediately spoon topping into 6 to 8 mounds on hot filling. Sprinkle with the 1 teaspoon sugar. ▼ **Bake** in a 400° oven for 20 to 25 minutes or till a toothpick inserted into topping comes out clean. Serve warm with ice cream or sweetened whipped cream.

Plum-Citrus Frozen Yogurt

Makes 6 to 8 servings

This easy-to-make dessert packs lots of sweet plum flavor. For homemade frozen yogurt with a pink blush, pick red-skinned plums, such as Santa Rosa or Red Beaut.

⅔ cup sugar
1 envelope unflavored gelatin
1½ cups milk
1 8-ounce carton orange low-fat yogurt

1 teaspoon vanilla
▼
5 *or* 6 medium plums, pitted and quartered (about 3 cups)

Per Serving

Calories	197
Protein	5 g
Carbohydrate	42 g
Total Fat	2 g
Saturated Fat	1 g
Cholesterol	6 mg
Sodium	54 mg
Potassium	328 mg

In a small saucepan stir together the sugar and gelatin; stir in milk. Cook and stir over low heat till gelatin is dissolved. Remove from heat; stir in yogurt and vanilla. ▼ **In a blender** container combine plum pieces and gelatin mixture. Cover and blend till nearly smooth. Pour the plum mixture into a 9x9x2-inch pan. Cover and freeze about 4 hours or till almost firm. ▼ **Break the frozen** plum mixture into chunks. Transfer the chunks to a large, chilled mixer bowl. Beat with an electric mixer on medium speed till smooth but not melted. Return quickly to the cold pan. Cover and freeze about 3 hours or till firm. ▼ **Before serving,** let frozen yogurt stand at room temperature about 10 to 15 minutes to soften.

PLUMS

Rosy Plum Sauce

Makes 6 to 8 servings (about 2 cups)

Per Serving

Calories	220
Protein	3 g
Carbohydrate	37 g
Total Fat	8 g
Saturated Fat	5 g
Cholesterol	30 mg
Sodium	58 mg
Potassium	297 mg

¼ **cup sugar**
1 **teaspoon cornstarch**
5 **or 6 medium plums,**
   pitted and sliced
   (2½ cups)

2 **tablespoons water**
▼
Vanilla ice cream
Plum wedges

In a medium saucepan combine the sugar and cornstarch. Stir in the sliced plums and water. Bring to boiling, stirring occasionally. Reduce heat and simmer sauce, covered, for 6 to 8 minutes or till desired consistency. ▼ **Cool the sauce** slightly. Serve warm sauce over vanilla ice cream and top with fresh plum wedges.

If your plums aren't fully ripe, ripen them at room temperature, then refrigerate. Use the plums in 3 to 5 days.

Selecting Summer Fruits

A good rule of thumb is to select plump fruit that "gives" when lightly pressed. Avoid shriveled, discolored, or bruised fruit (although slightly bruised is fine for canning.)
Apricots, peaches, pears, plums nectarines, and melons shipped long distances are picked before fully ripe; locally grown fruit may be fully ripe. If these fruits are still firm when you buy them, place them in a paper bag, loosely closed, and keep them on your kitchen counter until they are slightly soft to the touch. Ripe fruit also smells fragrant. Store ripe fruit, uncovered, in the refrigerator for 3 to 5 days.
Berries and cherries are picked ripe so they require extra-careful handling. Lightly cover and refrigerate them as soon as you arrive home. Rinse them just before eating.

PLUMS

Plum Strudel

Makes 12 to 16 servings

This ultra-flaky strudel, made with frozen phyllo dough, is utterly delicious.

1 pound plums (6 medium), pitted and chopped (2½ cups)
½ cup snipped, dried apricots
½ cup chopped almonds, toasted
¼ cup raisins
¾ cup sugar
1 teaspoon ground cinnamon

▼

10 to 12 18x12-inch sheets frozen phyllo dough, thawed
⅓ cup margarine or butter, melted

▼

1 slightly beaten egg white
1 tablespoon water

▼

Powdered Sugar Glaze or 2 tablespoons powdered sugar

Per Serving

Calories	291
Protein	4 g
Carbohydrate	43 g
Total Fat	13 g
Saturated Fat	2 g
Cholesterol	18 mg
Sodium	164 mg
Potassium	231 mg

For plum filling, in a medium mixing bowl combine plums, dried apricots, almonds, and raisins. Add sugar and cinnamon; gently toss till mixed. Set filling aside. Lightly grease a 15x10x1-inch baking pan; set aside. ▼ **Cover a large surface** with a cloth; flour cloth. Unfold phyllo dough. Stack *two* sheets of phyllo on the floured cloth. (Do not brush margarine or butter between sheets.) Arrange another stack of *two* sheets on the cloth, overlapping the stacks 2 inches. Add 3 or 4 more stacks, forming a rectangle about 40x20 inches (stagger stacks so all seams are not down the middle). Trim to a 40x20-inch rectangle. Brush with melted margarine or butter. ▼ **To assemble strudel,** beginning 4 inches from a short side of the dough, spoon the plum filling in a 4-inch-wide band across the dough. Using the cloth underneath the dough as a guide, gently lift the 4-inch piece of dough and lay it over the plum filling. Then slowly and evenly lift cloth and roll up the dough and plum filling, jelly-roll style, into a tight roll. If necessary, cut off excess dough from ends to within 1 inch of the plum filling. Fold ends under to seal.
▼ **Carefully transfer** the strudel roll to the prepared baking pan. Slightly curve the roll to form a crescent shape. In a small mixing bowl stir together the egg white and water. Brush the top of the strudel with the egg white mixture. ▼ **Bake** in a 350° oven 35 to 40 minutes or till golden. Carefully remove strudel from pan. Cool. Drizzle with Powdered Sugar Glaze or sift powdered sugar over strudel before serving.

Plum and Nectarine Pie

Makes 8 servings

Per Serving

Calories	310
Protein	4 g
Carbohydrate	59 g
Total Fat	7 g
Saturated Fat	2 g
Cholesterol	000 mg
Sodium	68 mg
Potassium	250 mg

¾ **cup sugar**
3 **tablespoons all-purpose flour**
1 **teaspoon vanilla**
¾ **teaspoon ground cinnamon**
¼ **teaspoon ground nutmeg**
8 **medium plums, pitted and sliced (4 cups)**
2 **medium nectarines, pitted and thinly sliced (2 cups)**

▼

2 **cups all-purpose flour**
¼ **teaspoon salt**
⅔ **cup shortening or lard**
6 **to 7 tablespoons cold water**

▼

Milk
Cinnamon-sugar

For the cinnamon-sugar topping, mix 1 tablespoon sugar with ¼ teaspoon ground cinnamon.

For filling, in a large mixing bowl stir together sugar, the 3 tablespoons flour, vanilla, cinnamon, and nutmeg. Add the plum and nectarine slices; gently toss plums and nectarines till coated. Set filling aside.
▼ **For pastry,** in a large mixing bowl stir together the 2 cups flour and salt. Using a pastry blender, cut in the shortening or lard till pieces are the size of small peas. Sprinkle *1 tablespoon* of the water over part of the flour mixture, then gently toss with a fork. Push moistened dough to the side of the bowl. Repeat, using 1 tablespoon of water at a time, till all is moistened. Divide dough in half. Form each half into a ball.
▼ **On a lightly floured surface,** use your hands to slightly flatten *one* ball of dough. Roll dough from center to edges, forming a 12-inch circle. Wrap the pastry around the rolling pin. Unroll onto a 9-inch pie plate. Ease pastry into the pie plate, being careful not to stretch it.
▼ **For top crust,** repeat rolling with remaining dough. Transfer the filling to the pastry-lined pie plate. Trim the bottom pastry even with rim of pie plate. Cut slits in top crust to allow steam to escape. Place top crust on filling. Trim top crust ½-inch beyond edge of plate. Fold top crust under bottom crust; flute edge. ▼ **Brush** with milk and sprinkle with cinnamon-sugar. To prevent overbrowning, cover the edge of pie with foil. ▼ **Bake** in a 375° oven for 25 minutes. Remove the foil. Bake for 20 to 25 minutes more or till top is golden. Cool pie on a wire rack.

Nectarine Blintze Quesadillas

Makes 4 servings

A blintze is a dessert of thin pancakes rolled around a fruit filling. Instead of a pancake, we made a quicker version out of flour tortillas.

1 medium nectarine, quartered
4 ounces cream cheese, softened
½ cup ricotta cheese
¼ cup sifted powdered sugar
1 teaspoon vanilla
¼ teaspoon ground cinnamon

4 8-inch flour tortillas
2 medium nectarines, pitted and thinly sliced (2 cups)
▼
2 tablespoons margarine *or* butter, melted
1 tablespoon sugar
¼ teaspoon ground cinnamon

Per Serving

Calories	378
Protein	9 g
Carbohydrate	41 g
Total Fat	20 g
Saturated Fat	9 g
Cholesterol	41 mg
Sodium	190 mg
Potassium	293 mg

For filling, in a blender container or food processor bowl place the nectarine quarters. Cover and blend or process till smooth. Add cream cheese, ricotta cheese, powdered sugar, vanilla, and ¼ teaspoon cinnamon. Cover and blend or process till combined. Spread filling evenly on each flour tortilla to within ½-inch of the edges. Arrange sliced nectarines over half of filling on each tortilla. ▼ **In a large skillet** or griddle cook tortillas, 1 at a time, filling-side-up, over medium-high heat for 1 to 2 minutes or till heated through and tortilla is lightly browned. With a spatula, fold tortillas in half to cover nectarine slices. Remove from skillet. Cover and keep warm while cooking remaining tortillas. ▼ **To serve,** brush each quesadilla with margarine or butter. Combine sugar and ¼ teaspoon cinnamon. Sprinkle cinnamon-sugar mixture on each quesadilla. Cut each quesadilla in thirds.

NECTARINES

Country Nectarine-Berry Pie

Makes 8 servings

Per Serving

Calories	259
Protein	3 g
Carbohydrate	38 g
Total Fat	11 g
Saturated Fat	3 g
Cholesterol	2 mg
Sodium	85 mg
Potassium	196 mg

½ **cup sugar**
1 **tablespoon all-purpose flour**
½ **teaspoon ground cinnamon**
¼ **teaspoon ground nutmeg**
4 **medium nectarines, pitted and thinly sliced (4 cups)**
1 **teaspoon lemon juice**

▼

Pastry for Single-Crust Pie (see recipe, page 163)
1 **cup red raspberries, blueberries, *or* blackberries**

▼

¼ **cup crushed vanilla wafers (5 or 6 vanilla wafers)**
1 **tablespoon chopped macadamia nuts *or* almonds**
2 **teaspoons margarine *or* butter, melted**
Milk

▼

Vanilla ice cream (optional)

We gave this pie a country look by enclosing the fruit filling in a rustic looking pastry bundle.

In a large mixing bowl stir together the sugar, flour, cinnamon, and nutmeg. Add nectarines and lemon juice; gently toss till nectarines are coated. ▼ **Prepare Pastry** for Single-Crust Pie as directed, *except* roll dough into 13-inch circle. Transfer dough to an ungreased 12-inch pizza pan or a 15x10x1-inch baking pan. Trim pastry to edge of pizza pan or to a 12-inch circle. Stir raspberries, blueberries, or blackberries into nectarine mixture. Mound fruit mixture in the center of the pastry, leaving about a 2-inch border. Fold the border up over the fruit mixture. ▼ **In a small mixing bowl** stir together crushed vanilla wafers, chopped macadamia nuts or almonds, and margarine or butter. Sprinkle crumb mixture atop the fruit. Brush pastry with milk. To prevent overbrowning, cover the crumb topping with foil. ▼ **Bake** in a 375° oven for 25 minutes. Remove foil. Bake for 15 to 20 minutes more or till the crust is golden. Cool in the pan on a wire rack. Serve warm or cool, with ice cream, if desired.

Chocolate Ravioli with Cherry-Orange Sauce

Makes 8 servings

Per Serving

Calories	286
Protein	8 g
Carbohydrate	44 g
Total Fat	10 g
Saturated Fat	5 g
Cholesterol	80 mg
Sodium	117 mg
Potassium	283 mg

Homemade Chocolate Ravioli Dough
1 medium orange
▼
⅔ cup ricotta cheese
2 tablespoons sugar
▼
⅓ cup sugar

4 teaspoons cornstarch
¼ cup water
3 cups pitted tart red cherries
1 tablespoon kirsch *or* orange liqueur
▼
Whipped cream

If you've never eaten dessert pasta, you're in for a special treat.

Prepare Homemade Chocolate Ravioli Dough. Finely shred *1 teaspoon* orange peel. Peel and section orange; set aside. ▼ **For filling,** combine ricotta cheese, the 2 tablespoons sugar, and orange peel. Set aside. ▼ **On a lightly floured surface** roll out pasta till ⅟₁₆ inch thick. Cut into 2-inch-wide strips. Place about *1 teaspoon* of filling at 1-inch intervals on 1 strip. Moisten pasta around filling by brushing it with water. Lay a second strip of dough on top; seal dough around each mound of filling. To separate ravioli, cut halfway between mounds of filling with a fluted pastry wheel or sharp knife. (Or, cut dough at angles to make triangles, as pictured on opposite page.) Repeat with remaining dough and filling. ▼ **Cook ravioli** in boiling water for 6 to 8 minutes or till tender. Drain. ▼ **Meanwhile,** for sauce, in a medium saucepan combine the ⅓ cup sugar and cornstarch. Stir in water and cherries. Cook and stir till thickened and bubbly. Cook and stir for 2 minutes more. Remove from heat. Stir in kirsch or orange liqueur and reserved orange sections. ▼ **To serve,** divide ravioli among 8 dessert plates. Spoon sauce over ravioli. Dollop with whipped cream.

Homemade Chocolate Ravioli Dough

In a large mixing bowl stir together 1¾ cups *all-purpose flour,* ¼ cup *unsweetened cocoa powder,* 2 tablespoons *sugar,* and ¼ teaspoon *salt.* Make a well in the center of the dry ingredients. In a small mixing bowl stir together 2 beaten *eggs,* ⅓ cup *water,* and 1 teaspoon *cooking oil.* Add to the flour mixture and mix well. Turn dough out onto a well-floured surface. Knead till dough is smooth and elastic (8 to 10 minutes total). Cover and let rest for 10 minutes.

CHERRIES

Black Cherry Sorbet

Makes 10 servings (5 cups)

Make this champagne sorbet ahead and keep on hand for unexpected celebrations.

5 cups pitted dark sweet
    cherries
1½ cups water

▼

1 cup sugar
1 cup champagne
2 teaspoons finely
    shredded lemon peel

Per Serving

Calories	143
Protein	1 g
Carbohydrate	32 g
Total Fat	1 g
Saturated Fat	0 g
Cholesterol	0 mg
Sodium	1 mg
Potassium	170 mg

In a blender container or food processor bowl combine cherries and *1 cup* of the water. Cover and blend or process till pureed. Strain cherry mixture through a sieve, discarding pulp. ▼ **In a bowl** combine strained cherry mixture, remaining water, sugar, champagne, and lemon peel, stirring till sugar dissolves. Pour into a 13x9x2-inch baking pan. Cover and freeze about 4 hours or till almost firm. Break the frozen mixture into chunks. ▼ **Transfer chunks** to a large, chilled mixer bowl. Beat with an electric mixer on medium speed till smooth but not melted. Return quickly to the cold pan. Cover and freeze for 6 to 8 hours or till sorbet is firm.

By freezing fresh cherries when they're available in late spring or early summer, you can enjoy them all year long. Rinse and dry the cherries (a pound of whole

Freezing Cherries

cherries is 3 cups). Pit them, if desired. Place the cherries in freezer bags or freezer containers, leaving a ½-inch headspace. Freeze the cherries for up to 12 months.

CHERRIES

Glazed Cherry Pie

Makes 8 servings

1¼ to 1½ cups sugar
2 tablespoons quick-cooking tapioca
5 cups pitted tart red cherries
Few drops almond extract
▼
Pastry for Double-Crust Pie

▼
¼ cup sifted powdered sugar
1 teaspoon cherry brandy *or* milk
¼ teaspoon almond extract

This classic summer pie works great with frozen cherries, too, but you'll have to increase the amount of time the cherries stand with the sugar and tapioca to about 60 minutes. Also, increase the cooking time to 50 minutes covered with foil and then bake for 20 to 30 minutes more without the foil.

In a large mixing bowl stir together the sugar and tapioca. Add cherries and the few drops almond extract; gently toss till cherries are coated. Let stand about 15 minutes or till syrup forms, stirring occasionally. ▼ **Prepare and roll out Pastry** for Double-Crust Pie as directed. Line a 9-inch pie plate with half of the pastry. Stir cherry mixture; transfer to the pastry-lined pie plate. Trim the bottom pastry to edge of pie plate. Cut slits in the top crust. Place top crust on filling. Trim top crust ½ inch beyond edge of plate. Fold top crust under bottom pastry. Seal and crimp edge of pastry. To prevent overbrowning, cover edge of pie with foil. Bake in a 375° oven for 25 minutes. Remove foil. Bake for 25 to 35 minute more or till top is golden. ▼ **For glaze,** in a small mixing bowl combine powdered sugar, cherry brandy or milk, and the ¼ teaspoon almond extract. If necessary, stir in additional cherry brandy or milk till of drizzling consistency. Drizzle glaze over hot pie. Cool pie on a wire rack.

Pastry for Double-Crust Pie

In a large mixing bowl stir together 2 cups *all-purpose flour* and ½ teaspoon *salt*. Using a pastry blender, cut in ⅔ cup *shortening or lard* till pieces are the size of small peas. Sprinkle 6 to 7 tablespoons *cold water,* 1 tablespoon at a time, over mixture, tossing with a fork after each addition till all is moistened. Divide dough in half. Form each half into a ball. ▼ **On a lightly floured surface,** use your hands to slightly flatten one ball of dough. Roll dough from center to edges, forming a 12-inch circle. Wrap the pastry around the rolling pin. Unroll onto a 9-inch pie plate. Ease pastry into the pie plate, being careful not to stretch it. For top crust, roll remaining dough as directed above.

CHERRIES

Cherry Pastry Fingers
Makes 18

Fresh cherries are meant to be enjoyed as soon as possible. Refrigerate them, covered, for up to 4 days.

1 cup margarine *or* butter
1 8-ounce package cream cheese, softened
2 cups all-purpose flour
2 tablespoons sugar
¼ teaspoon salt
▼
3 tablespoons sugar
4 teaspoons cornstarch
1 tablespoon water

4 cups pitted tart red cherries
1 teaspoon finely shredded lemon peel
▼
1 cup sifted powdered sugar
¼ teaspoon almond extract
Milk

Per Serving

Calories	234
Protein	3 g
Carbohydrate	23 g
Total Fat	15 g
Saturated Fat	4 g
Cholesterol	14 mg
Sodium	187 mg
Potassium	79 mg

For pastry, in a large mixing bowl beat margarine or butter and cream cheese with an electric mixer on mediuim to high speed till fluffy. Stir in flour, the 2 tablespoons sugar, and salt. Divide dough in half. Cover and chill dough for one hour or till easy to handle. (Dough may be chilled overnight.) ▼ **For filling,** in a large saucepan stir together the 3 tablespoons sugar, cornstarch, and water. Add cherries. Cook and stir over medium heat till thickened and bubbly. Cook and stir for 2 minutes more. Stir in lemon peel. Remove filling from heat. Cool completely. ▼ **On a lightly floured surface,** roll each portion of dough into a 15x10½-inch rectangle. With a knife, cut each rectangle into nine 5x3½-inch rectangles. Spoon about *2 tablespoons* of the cherry filling lengthwise down the center of each small rectangle to within ½ inch of each end. Starting from one of the long sides, lift dough up and over cherries, then lift dough from other long side over center; seal. Press ends with the tines of a fork to seal. Place pastry fingers, seam side down, on a foil-lined cookie sheet. Press ends with the tines of a fork again to seal. ▼ **Bake** in a 375° oven about 12 minutes or till lightly brown. Remove from cookie sheet. Cool on a wire rack. Meanwhile, for icing, in a small mixing bowl stir together the powdered sugar, almond extract, and enough milk (1 to 2 tablespoons) to make an icing of drizzling consistency. Drizzle icing over pastry fingers.

MELON

Melon Juleps
Makes 4 to 6 servings

Per Serving

Calories	174
Protein	2 g
Carbohydrate	36 g
Total Fat	0 g
Saturated Fat	0 g
Cholesterol	0 mg
Sodium	27 mg
Potassium	665 mg

⅓ **cup water**

⅓ **cup sugar**

3 **tablespoons snipped fresh mint** *or* **1 teaspoon dried mint, crushed**

¼ **cup rum**

1 **tablespoon lemon juice** *or* **lime juice**

▼

6 **cups desired melon balls (watermelon, honeydew melon, cantaloupe,** *or* **casaba)**

Fresh mint

For a pretty presentation, serve this refreshing summer dessert in stemmed glasses.

For sugar syrup, in a small saucepan combine the water, sugar, and mint. Bring to boiling; stirring constantly. Remove from heat and strain to remove mint. Stir in rum and lemon or lime juice. Cool syrup thoroughly. ▼ **In a large serving bowl** combine the melon balls and cooled syrup. Cover and chill for 2 to 4 hours. To serve, spoon melon balls and syrup into dessert dishes. Garnish with mint.

Chicken-Melon Salad with Chutney Dressing

Makes 4 main-dish servings

An intriguing flavor combo—chutney dressing over cooked chicken, juicy honeydew chunks, and dark sweet cherries.

¼ cup chutney
2 tablespoons salad oil
2 tablespoons vinegar
2 teaspoons Dijon-style mustard
2 teaspoons soy sauce
¼ teaspoon toasted sesame oil
⅛ teaspoon crushed red pepper
1 small clove garlic, halved
▼
2½ cups cooked chicken *or* turkey cut into bite-size strips (about 12 ounces)
2 cups honeydew melon *or* cantaloupe chunks

½ cup canned sliced water chestnuts, drained and halved
½ cup halved pitted dark, sweet cherries *or* halved seedless red grapes
⅓ cup cashew halves
1 green onion, sliced (2 tablespoons)
▼
Red *or* white salad savoy leaves *or* savoy cabbage leaves
1 tablespoon snipped fresh chives

Per Serving

Calories	395
Protein	28 g
Carbohydrate	30 g
Total Fat	19 g
Saturated Fat	4 g
Cholesterol	76 mg
Sodium	331 mg
Potassium	683 mg

For dressing, in a blender container or food processor bowl combine chutney, salad oil, vinegar, mustard, soy sauce, toasted sesame oil, red pepper, and garlic. Cover and blend or process till pureed. Set dressing aside. ▼ **In a large salad bowl** combine chicken or turkey strips, melon chunks, water chestnuts, cherry or grape halves, cashews, and green onion. Pour dressing over salad. Toss lightly to coat. ▼ **Line four salad plates** with salad savoy or savoy cabbage leaves. Divide chicken mixture among the lettuce-lined plates. Sprinkle with the snipped chives.

MELON

Watermelon Daiquiris

Makes 4 (10-ounce) servings

Per Serving

Calories	234
Protein	1 g
Carbohydrate	35 g
Total Fat	0 g
Saturated Fat	0 g
Cholesterol	0 mg
Sodium	7 mg
Potassium	155 mg

2½ cups cubed watermelon, seeded
¾ cup light rum

1 6-ounce can frozen pink lemonade concentrate
20 to 24 ice cubes (3 to 4 cups)

In a blender container place *half* of the watermelon, *half* of the rum, and *half* of the lemonade concentrate. Cover and blend till smooth. With blender running, add *half* of the ice cubes, one at a time, through the opening in the lid. Blend till slushy. (If the mixture becomes too thick, add a little water.) Pour into 2 chilled wine glasses. Repeat with remaining ingredients. Serve immediately.

Save yourself alot of time by using a seedless watermelon when you make this refreshing rum drink.

Selecting Melons

Melons differ in appearance—shape, size, and interior and exterior color—as well as in flavor and texture. Look for melons with characteristics that match those listed here for each type.

Melon	Appearance	Interior Color	Flavor and Texture
Cantaloupe	Round; cream-colored netting over a yellowish green rind	Orange	Sweet, moist and juicy
Casaba	Globe-shaped with one pointed end; golden yellow rind with wrinkled appearance	Creamy white	Sweet, moist and juicy
Crenshaw	Oval; mottled green and yellow rind that is mostly smooth	Salmon	Rich, sweet and spicy taste; highly aromatic; moist and juicy
Honeydew	Round; smooth, waxy rind that is creamy white with a green to pale yellow cast	Pale green (sometimes pink, green, gold, or orange	Sweet; honey aroma; moist and juicy
Persian	Round; fine netting over a green to golden yellow rind	Salmon	Tastes like a mildly sweet cantaloupe; firm with buttery texture
Watermelon	Oblong, oval, or round; hard, smooth rind that is solid, striped, or mottled green	Deep pink to red (sometimes yellow)	Sweet, crisp and juicy

CHERRIES

Cherry-Berry Freezer Jam

Makes about 6 half-pints (ninety-six 1-tablespoon servings)

Per Serving

Calories	38
Protein	0 g
Carbohydrate	10 g
Total Fat	0 g
Saturated Fat	0 g
Cholesterol	0 mg
Sodium	1 mg
Potassium	8 mg

3 cups pitted tart red cherries
2 cups blueberries
4¼ cups sugar
2 tablespoons finely chopped crystallized ginger

▼
1 cup water
1 1¾-ounce package powdered fruit pectin

Halve cherries. Crush blueberries slightly. In a large bowl combine cherries, blueberries, sugar, and ginger. Let stand for 10 minutes. ▼ **Meanwhile,** in a small saucepan combine water and pectin. Bring to a full, rolling boil (a boil that cannot be stirred down). Boil hard for 1 minute, stirring constantly. Stir pectin mixture into fruit mixture. Stir constantly for 3 minutes. ▼ **Ladle at once** into jars or freezer containers, leaving a ½-inch headspace. Seal; label. Let stand at room temperature for 24 hours. Store jam up to 3 weeks in the refrigerator or 1 year in the freezer.

Crystallized ginger, also called candied ginger, is bits of gingerroot that are cooked in a sugar syrup, then coated with sugar. Look for it in the spice section of your supermarket.

155

FRUIT COMBO

Fruit Pizza

Makes 12 servings

This colorful dessert pizza will draw rave reviews from your family and friends.

½ cup margarine *or* butter
1 cup all-purpose flour
¼ cup sifted powdered
    sugar

▼

2 tablespoons sugar
2 tablespoons cornstarch
⅛ teaspoon ground mace
⅓ cup orange juice
½ cup currant jelly

▼

1 medium peach, peeled,
    pitted, and sliced (1 cup)
1 medium nectarine, pitted
    and sliced (1 cup)
1 cup sliced strawberries
½ cup blueberries
½ cup seedless green
    grapes, halved

Per Serving

Calories	184
Protein	2 g
Carbohydrate	28 g
Total Fat	8 g
Saturated Fat	1 g
Cholesterol	0 mg
Sodium	92 mg
Potassium	137 mg

For crust, in a small mixer bowl beat margarine or butter with an electric mixer on medium-high speed for 30 seconds. Gradually add flour and powdered sugar till well combined. Pat dough evenly over the bottom and up the sides of a 12-inch pizza pan. Bake in a 350° oven for 10 to 12 minutes or till golden. Cool completely on a wire rack. ▼ **Meanwhile,** for glaze, in a medium saucepan stir together the sugar, cornstarch, and mace. Stir in orange juice and currant jelly. Cook and stir over medium heat till thickened and bubbly. Cook and stir 2 minutes more. Cool slightly. ▼ **Spread** *half* of the glaze (about ⅔ cup) onto cooled crust. Arrange peach and nectarine slices around edge of crust, then arrange strawberries, working toward center of crust. Sprinkle all with blueberries and grapes. Drizzle remaining glaze over fruit. Chill up to 4 hours. Cut into wedges to serve.

FRUIT COMBO

Nectarine-Blueberry Bread

Makes 1 loaf (16 servings)

Per Serving

Calories	163
Protein	3 g
Carbohydrate	21 g
Total Fat	8 g
Saturated Fat	1 g
Cholesterol	27 mg
Sodium	141 mg
Potassium	92 mg

⅔ **cup chopped almonds**
1 **tablespoon sugar**
▼
1½ **cups all-purpose flour**
¾ **cup sugar**
2 **teaspoons baking powder**
½ **teaspoon ground allspice**
¼ **teaspoon baking soda**
¼ **teaspoon salt**
⅓ **cup margarine** *or* **butter, softened**

1 **teaspoon finely shredded orange peel**
¼ **cup orange juice**
2 **eggs**
1 **medium nectarine** *or* **peeled peach, pitted and coarsely chopped (¾ cup)**
½ **cup blueberries**

Serve this fruit-filled loaf, with a crackly, almond streusel topping, for breakfast or brunch, and watch it go fast.

Grease a 9x5x3-inch loaf pan; set aside. For streusel topping, in a small mixing bowl stir together ¼ *cup* of the almonds and the 1 tablespoon sugar; set topping aside. ▼ **In a large mixing bowl** stir together *1 cup* of the flour, the ¾ cup sugar, baking powder, allspice, baking soda, and salt. Add margarine or butter, orange peel, and orange juice. Beat with an electric mixer on low to medium speed about 30 seconds or till combined, then beat on high speed for 2 minutes. Add eggs and remaining flour. Beat on low speed just till combined. Carefully fold in chopped nectarine or peach, blueberries, and remaining almonds. Pour into prepared pan. Sprinkle the streusel topping over top of batter. ▼ **Bake** in a 350° oven for 55 to 60 minutes or till a wooden toothpick inserted near the center comes out clean. To prevent overbrowning, cover with foil the last 15 minutes, if necessary. Cool bread in pan on a wire rack for 10 minutes. Remove bread from pan and cool completely on the wire rack. Wrap and store overnight before slicing.

FRUIT COMBO

Couscous Fruit Salad with Ginger-Orange Dressing

Makes 4 to 6 servings

Instead of plums, peaches, and nectarines, you could make this fruit salad with oranges, grapes, and strawberries.

⅔ **cup water**
⅓ **cup couscous**
▼
1 **teaspoon finely shredded orange peel**
⅓ **cup orange juice**
2 **tablespoons salad oil**
1 **teaspoon grated gingerroot**
⅛ **teaspoon salt**
⅛ **teaspoon pepper**

▼
2 **plums, pitted and chopped (about 1 cup)**
1 **medium peach, peeled, pitted, and chopped (¾ cup)**
1 **medium nectarine, pitted and chopped (¾ cup)**
1 **green onion, thinly sliced (2 tablespoons)**
¼ **cup slivered almonds, toasted**

Per Serving

Calories	214
Protein	4 g
Carbohydrate	26 g
Total Fat	11 g
Saturated Fat	1 g
Cholesterol	0 mg
Sodium	70 mg
Potassium	293 mg

In a small saucepan bring water to boiling. Remove from heat and stir in couscous. Let stand, covered, for 5 minutes or till liquid is absorbed.
▼ **Meanwhile,** for dressing, in a screw-top jar combine orange peel, orange juice, salad oil, gingerroot, salt, and pepper. Cover and shake well. Set dressing aside. ▼ **In a medium mixing bowl** combine couscous, plums, peaches, nectarines, and green onion. Shake dressing well; pour over salad mixture. Toss lightly to coat. Cover and chill for 4 to 24 hours. Before serving, stir in toasted almonds.

If you're lucky enough to live in an area where nuts are native, you'll probably find them at your local farmer's market. Otherwise, you can sometimes order nuts from mail-order sources and specialty stores.

Black Walnuts: The native North American black walnut has a very hard, thick, rough, black shell. The nut itself is smaller, has a darker skin and richer, more intense flavor than the English walnut. Black walnuts are difficult to shell. Store shelled nuts in an airtight container in the refrigerator and they'll stay fresh for 6 months. For longer storage, freeze shelled nuts for up to a year.

Hickory Nuts: This nut, the fruit of an American tree that grows wild in woods and forests, has a rounded, paneled, light tan shell. A close relative to the pecan, hickory nuts resemble small pecans and have a rich, oily flavor. Shelled nuts will keep in an airtight container in the refrigerator for up to 1 year and in the freezer at least 2 years.

Black Walnut-Chocolate Pie

Makes 8 servings

Per Serving

Calories	545
Protein	9 g
Carbohydrate	65 g
Total Fat	29 g
Saturated Fat	4 g
Cholesterol	80 mg
Sodium	215 mg
Potassium	184 mg

3 eggs
1 cup light corn syrup
½ cup sugar
⅓ cup margarine *or* butter, melted
1 cup black walnut pieces *or* hickory nut pieces

▼
Pastry for Single-Crust Pie (see recipe, page 163)
½ cup miniature semisweet chocolate pieces
▼
Whipped cream (optional)

For filling, in a bowl lightly beat eggs *just till combined.* Stir in corn syrup, sugar, and melted margarine. Mix well. Stir in black walnuts. Set filling aside. ▼ **Prepare Pastry** for Single-Crust Pie. On a lightly floured surface, slightly flatten dough. Roll dough from center to edges, forming a 12-inch circle. Wrap pastry around the rolling pin. Unroll onto a 9-inch pie plate. Ease pastry into pie plate, being careful not to stretch it. Trim pastry to ½ inch beyond edge of plate. Fold under extra pastry; crimp edge. Sprinkle chocolate pieces over bottom of pastry shell. With pastry shell on oven rack, pour filling into shell. ▼ **To prevent** over-browning, cover edge of pie with foil. Bake in a 350° oven 20 minutes. Remove foil. Bake 20 to 25 minutes more or till a knife inserted near center of pie comes out clean. Cool. Store, covered, in the refrigerator. Dollop with whipped cream before serving, if desired.

White Chocolate Bavarian Creme with Strawberry Glacé

Makes 6 servings

To make straw-berry fans, use a sharp knife to cut a berry into thin, lengthwise slices (do not cut all the way through the stem end). Using your fingers, fan out the strawberry.

½ cup sugar
1 envelope unflavored gelatin
1⅓ cups milk
3 slightly beaten egg yolks
1 6-ounce package white baking bar, chopped

½ cup whipping cream
▼
Strawberry Glacé
▼
6 strawberry fans

Per Serving	
Calories	416
Protein	6 g
Carbohydrate	56 g
Total Fat	20 g
Saturated Fat	11 g
Cholesterol	138 mg
Sodium	66 mg
Potassium	285 mg

In a medium saucepan combine sugar and gelatin. Stir in the milk and egg yolks. Cook and stir over medium heat till mixture thickens slightly and gelatin dissolves. Stir in chopped white baking bar just till melted. Remove saucepan from the heat. Pour the gelatin mixture into a large mixing bowl. Chill about one hour or till gelatin mixture is the consistency of corn syrup, stirring occasionally. Remove gelatin mixture from the refrigerator. Beat whipping cream till soft peaks form (tips curl); fold whipped cream into the gelatin mixture. ▼ **Divide Strawberry Glacé** evenly among six ungreased 6-ounce custard cups. Carefully spoon the whipped cream mixture evenly onto the Strawberry Glacé in custard cups. Chill for 4 to 24 hours or till firm. ▼ **To serve,** loosen sides of gelatin mixture from custard cups with a narrow spatula. Unmold each custard cup onto the center of a dessert plate. For garnish, top each with a strawberry fan.

Strawberry Glacé

Remove stems from 1 cup *strawberries*. In a blender container or food processor bowl combine strawberries and ½ cup *water*. Cover and blend or process till smooth. If necessary, add enough additional *water* to equal 1 cup. In a medium saucepan combine ½ cup *sugar* and 1 tablespoon *cornstarch*. Stir in pureed strawberry mixture. Cook and stir over medium heat till mixture is thickened and bubbly. Cook and stir for 2 minutes more. Stir in 2 drops *red food coloring*, if desired. Cool for 10 minutes without stirring. Makes 1 cup.

STRAWBERRIES

Lemon-Poppy Seed Strawberry Shortcake

Makes 10 servings

6 cups sliced strawberries
¼ cup sugar (optional)
▼
2 cups all-purpose flour
1 tablespoon baking powder
½ teaspoon cream of tartar
¼ teaspoon baking soda
½ cup margarine *or* butter
¾ cup buttermilk *or* sour milk

2 tablespoons poppy seed
1 teaspoon finely shredded lemon peel
▼
⅔ cup whipping cream
8 ounces mascarpone cheese *or* soft-style cream cheese
¾ cup sifted powdered sugar
½ teaspoon finely shredded lemon peel

This yummy, biscuitlike shortcake is split and layered with juicy berries, and a whipped topping that uses mascarpone (*mask car PONY*), cheese as a base. Look for it at larger supermarkets, cheese shops, or Italian specialty stores.

In a medium mixing bowl stir together strawberries and, if desired, the ¼ cup sugar. Set aside. ▼ **For the shortcake,** in a medium mixing bowl combine the flour, baking powder, cream of tartar, and baking soda. Cut in the margarine or butter till mixture resembles coarse crumbs. Make a well in the center; add the buttermilk, poppy seed, and the 1 teaspoon lemon peel all at once. Stir just till dough clings together. ▼ **On a lightly floured surface,** knead dough gently for 10 to 12 strokes. Pat dough into an 8-inch circle on a baking sheet. Bake in a 450° oven for 15 to 18 minutes or till golden. ▼ **Meanwhile,** for mascarpone cheese mixture, in a medium mixing bowl beat the whipping cream with an electric mixer on low speed just till soft peaks form. Add the mascarpone cheese, powdered sugar, and the ½ teaspoon lemon peel; beat till fluffy (mixture will thicken as it is beaten). ▼ **Split shortcake** into 2 layers. Place bottom layer on serving platter. Spread *half* of the mascarpone cheese mixture atop the bottom layer of shortcake. Spoon some of the strawberries onto cheese layer. Add top layer of shortcake. Repeat cheese and strawberry layers. Pass any remaining strawberries. Cut into wedges. Serve immediately.

STRAWBERRIES

Strawberry-Banana Cream Pie

Makes 8 servings

Per Serving

Calories	368
Protein	6 g
Carbohydrate	42 g
Total Fat	20 g
Saturated Fat	7 g
Cholesterol	78 mg
Sodium	119 mg
Potassium	324 mg

Pastry for Single-Crust Pie
¼ cup finely chopped almonds, toasted
▼
½ cup sugar
2 tablespoons cornstarch
1¾ cups milk
2 beaten egg yolks
1 tablespoon margarine *or* butter

½ teaspoon vanilla
▼
2 medium bananas
2 teaspoons lemon juice
2 cups sliced strawberries
▼
½ cup whipping cream
1 tablespoons sugar
¼ teaspoon almond extract

Layers of fresh strawberries between the sliced bananas and custard add a new twist to this perennial family favorite.

Prepare Pastry for Single-Crust pie *except* stir almonds into flour mixture. On a floured surface, roll pastry to a 12-inch circle. Wrap pastry around rolling pin. Unroll onto a 9-inch pie plate. Ease pastry into pie plate. ▼ **Trim pastry** to ½ inch beyond edge of plate. Fold under extra pastry. Crimp edge of pastry. *Do not prick pastry.* Line the pastry shell with a double thickness of foil. Bake in a 450° oven 8 minutes. Remove foil. Bake 4 to 5 minutes more or till set and dry. Cool. ▼ **For filling,** in a saucepan mix the ½ cup sugar and cornstarch. Gradually stir in milk. Cook and stir till bubbly. Cook and stir 2 minutes more. Remove from heat. Stir about 1 cup of the hot mixture into the beaten egg yolks. Return all to saucepan. Bring to a gentle boil. Cook and stir 2 minutes more. Remove from heat. Stir in margarine and vanilla. Cover surface with plastic wrap. ▼ **Slice bananas** ¼-inch-thick; toss with lemon juice. (You should have about 1¼ cups). Spread half the hot filling evenly into pastry shell. Arrange half the bananas and strawberries on top. Top with remaining filling, bananas, and strawberries. Cover; chill 1 to 6 hours. ▼ **Before serving,** beat the whipping cream, 1 tablespoon sugar, and almond extract till stiff peaks form. Pipe or dollop onto pie.

Pastry for Single-Crust Pie

Mix 1¼ cups *all-purpose flour* and ¼ teaspoon *salt*. Cut in ⅓ cup *shortening or lard* till pieces are the size of small peas. Sprinkle 3 to 4 tablespoons *cold water,* 1 tablespoon at a time, over mixture, tossing with a fork after each addition till all is moistened. Form dough into a ball.

STRAWBERRIES

Soda Fountain Pie

Makes 10 servings

This refreshing strawberry ice-cream pie has a unique crust made with crushed ice cream cones.

1½ cups crushed sugar ice-cream cones (one 5-ounce package, about 12 cones)
½ cup margarine *or* butter, melted
¼ cup sugar
3½ cups strawberries

▼
1 quart vanilla ice cream, softened
⅓ cup malted milk powder
1 11.75-ounce jar hot fudge ice cream topping (about 1½ cups)

Per Serving

Calories	424
Protein	6 g
Carbohydrate	57 g
Total Fat	20 g
Saturated Fat	9 g
Cholesterol	25 mg
Sodium	219 mg
Potassium	366 mg

In a small bowl combine crushed cones, margarine or butter, and sugar. Press onto the bottom and 1 inch up the sides of a 9-inch springform pan or into a 10-inch pie plate; set aside. Place *3 cups* of the strawberries in a blender container. Cover and blend till smooth (you should have 1½ cups). Chop remaining strawberries. ▼ **In a large bowl** stir together strawberry puree, chopped strawberries, ice cream, and malted milk powder. Pour into prepared crust. Cover and freeze for 8 hours or till firm. Spread fudge topping over pie; freeze at least 2 hours more.
▼ **To serve,** let pie stand at room temperature for 30 minutes before cutting into wedges.

STRAWBERRIES

Strawberry Ice Cream With Cinnamon Cones

Makes about 3 quarts ice cream

Per Serving
(Ice Cream
And Cone)

Calories	302
Protein	5 g
Carbohydrate	30 g
Total Fat	19 g
Saturated Fat	10 g
Cholesterol	103 mg
Sodium	89 mg
Potassium	166 mg

2 **cups sugar**
2 **envelopes unflavored**
    gelatin
6 **cups half-and-half *or* light**
    cream
6 **beaten eggs**
2 **cups whipping cream**
3 **tablespoons vanilla**

▼

3 **to 4 cups sliced straw-**
    berries
¼ **cup sugar**

▼

Cinnamon Ice-Cream Cones

Dress up your homemade ice-cream cones by dipping the top and bottom into melted chocolate.

In a large saucepan combine the 2 cups sugar and the gelatin. Stir in half-and-half or light cream. Cook and stir over medium heat till mixture almost boils and sugar dissolves. Stir about 1 cup of the hot mixture into the beaten eggs; return all to saucepan. Cook and stir for 2 minutes more. *Do not boil.* Stir in whipping cream and vanilla. Cool. ▼
In a small mixing bowl combine sliced strawberries and the ¼ cup sugar. Use a pastry blender or potato masher to slightly crush the strawberries; stir into cooled custard. ▼ **Freeze** in a 4- or 5-quart ice-cream freezer according to manufacturer's directions. Serve in Cinnamon Ice-Cream Cones.

Cinnamon Ice Cream Cones

In a medium mixing bowl beat 1 *egg white* till soft peaks form. Gradually add ¼ cup *sugar;* beating till stiff peaks form. Combine ¼ cup *all-purpose flour* and ½ teaspoon *ground cinnamon;* stir into beaten egg white. Stir in 2 tablespoons melted and cooled *margarine or butter.*
▼ **Generously grease** two 5-inch circles on a cookie sheet. Drop a small mound of batter (1 level measuring tablespoonful) onto each greased spot. Spread with the back of a spoon into 4-inch circles.
▼ **Bake** in a 350° oven for 6 to 8 minutes or till done. Immediately loosen and roll around a metal cone. Slip the cookies off the cone and cool. (*Or,* use a towel or hot pad to press cookie over the bottoms of greased custard cups.) Repeat with remaining batter, using a clean, greased circle on cookie sheet for each. Makes 8 to 10.

Blueberry-Rhubarb Crumble

Makes 6 servings

Warm-from-the-oven, old-fashioned fruit desserts are everyone's favorite. Serve this one with whipped cream or light cream.

1½ **cups rolled oats**
⅔ **cup packed brown sugar**
½ **cup all-purpose flour**
½ **cup margarine *or* butter**

▼

3 **cups blueberries**

2 **cups rhubarb cut into 1-inch pieces**
½ **cup sugar**
2 **tablespoons all-purpose flour**

Per Serving

Calories	406
Protein	3 g
Carbohydrate	65 g
Total Fat	16
Saturated Fat	3 g
Cholesterol	0 mg
Sodium	193 mg
Potassium	310 mg

For crust, in a large mixing bowl combine the oats, brown sugar, and the ½ cup flour. With a pastry blender or fork, cut in the margarine or butter till mixture resembles coarse crumbs. Reserve ⅔ *cup* of the crumb mixture for topping. Pat remaining crumb mixture into the bottom of a greased 9x9x2-inch baking pan. Bake in a 350° oven for 10 to 15 minutes or till light brown. ▼ **Meanwhile,** for filling, in a large mixing bowl combine the blueberries and rhubarb. Add the sugar and the 2 tablespoons flour; toss to coat well. Spoon atop baked crust. Sprinkle with reserved crumb mixture. ▼ **Bake** in a 350° oven for 45 to 50 minutes or till golden. Serve warm.

White Chocolate-Blueberry Parfaits

Makes 6 servings

Per Serving

Calories	347
Protein	4 g
Carbohydrate	27 g
Total Fat	26 g
Saturated Fat	15 g
Cholesterol	127 mg
Sodium	55 mg
Potassium	196 mg

1 **6-ounce white baking bar, chopped**
½ **cup milk**
2 **beaten egg yolks**
1 **teaspoon vanilla**
t
1 **cup whipping cream**

▼
2 **cups blueberries**
   Whipped cream (optional)
   White baking bar curls (optional)

Do you have extra raspberries, blackberries, or strawberries? Any berry would be good layered with this sinfully rich white chocolate mixture.

In a heavy medium saucepan heat and stir white baking bar and milk over low heat till baking bar is melted. Gradually stir the white baking bar mixture into beaten egg yolks. Return mixture to saucepan. Bring to a gentle boil. Cook and stir for 2 minutes. Remove from the heat. Stir in vanilla. Pour into a large mixing bowl. Cool to room temperature, stirring occasionally. ▼ **Beat the whipping cream** till soft peaks form; fold whipped cream into the white chocolate mixture. Cover and chill for 4 to 24 hours before serving. ▼ **To serve,** layer white chocolate mixture over blueberries in parfait glasses. Garnish with additional whipped cream and white baking bar curls, if desired.

Blueberry Muffin Breakfast Cookies

Makes 18 cookies

Who said you can't eat cookies for breakfast? These cakelike cookies make a delicious start to any day.

1¼ cups all-purpose flour
½ cup packed brown sugar
1 teaspoon baking powder
½ teaspoon baking soda
¼ teaspoon ground cinnamon
⅛ teaspoon salt
⅓ cup margarine *or* butter
1 egg

⅓ cup milk
1 teaspoon finely shredded lemon peel *or* orange peel
¾ cup blueberries
¼ cup chopped walnuts

▼

Lemon Butter Frosting

Per Serving

Calories	130
Protein	2 g
Carbohydrate	19 g
Total Fat	6 g
Saturated Fat	1 g
Cholesterol	12 mg
Sodium	111 mg
Potassium	57 mg

Lightly grease a cookie sheet. (Repeat greasing cookie sheet for each batch.) Set aside. ▼ **In a large mixing bowl** combine flour, brown sugar, baking powder, baking soda, cinnamon, and salt. Using a pastry blender or a fork, cut in margarine or butter till pieces are the size of small peas. Make a well in the center of the dry ingredients. In a small mixing bowl combine egg, milk, and lemon peel or orange peel. Add all at once to the dry ingredients. Stir *just till moistened*. Fold in blueberries and walnuts. ▼ **Drop dough** from a rounded tablespoon 2 inches apart on prepared cookie sheet. Bake in a 375° oven for 10 to 12 minutes or till edges are set and lightly browned. Remove cookies from cookie sheet. Cool slightly on a wire rack. Frost with Lemon Butter Frosting. Serve warm.

Lemon Butter Frosting

In a small mixing bowl stir together 1 cup sifted *powdered sugar* and 1 tablespoon softened *margarine or butter*. Stir in ¼ teaspoon *finely shredded lemon peel or orange peel* and enough *water* to make of spreading consistency.

BLUEBERRIES

Blueberry-Ricotta Squares

Makes 16 servings

Per Serving

Calories	157
Protein	4 g
Carbohydrate	22 g
Total Fat	6 g
Saturated Fat	2 g
Cholesterol	46 mg
Sodium	98 mg
Potassium	63 mg

1 **cup all-purpose flour**
¾ **cup sugar**
1¼ **teaspoons baking powder**
¼ **teaspoon salt**
⅓ **cup milk**
¼ **cup shortening**
1 **egg**

½ **teaspoon vanilla**
1½ **cups blueberries**
▼
2 **eggs**
1¼ **cups ricotta cheese**
⅓ **cup sugar**
¼ **teaspoon vanilla**

This fresh blueberry recipe combines delicious cake and cheesecake layers for the best of both desserts.

In a small mixer bowl combine the flour, the ¾ cup sugar, baking powder, and salt. Add the milk, shortening, the 1 egg, and the ½ teaspoon vanilla. Beat with an electric mixer on low speed till combined. Beat on medium speed for 1 minute. Pour batter into a greased 9x9x2-inch baking pan and spread evenly. Sprinkle blueberries over batter.

▼ **In a medium mixing bowl** lightly beat the 2 eggs with a fork. Add ricotta cheese, the ⅓ cup sugar, and the ¼ teaspoon vanilla; beat till combined. Spoon ricotta mixture over blueberries and spread evenly.

▼ **Bake** in a 350° oven for 55 to 60 minutes or till a knife inserted near the center comes out clean. Cool. Cut into 16 squares. Cover and store in the refrigerator.

BLUEBERRIES

Blueberry Buckle Coffee Cake

Makes 10 servings

1½ cups all-purpose flour
1 cup packed brown sugar
1 teaspoon baking powder
½ teaspoon baking soda
¼ teaspoon salt
¼ teaspoon ground cinnamon
½ cup margarine *or* butter
1 slightly beaten egg

½ cup buttermilk *or* sour milk
1 teaspoon vanilla
▼
1½ cups blueberries
Crumb Topping
▼
1 tablespoon powdered sugar

If you don't have a 9-inch springform pan, you can bake this luscious breakfast cake in a 9x1½-inch round baking pan. Just go down to 1 cup of blueberries.

Grease a 9-inch springform pan. Line the bottom with waxed paper; grease the waxed paper. Flour the pan; set aside. ▼ **In a large mixing bowl** stir together flour, brown sugar, baking powder, baking soda, salt, and cinnamon. Using a pastry blender, cut in the margarine or butter till mixture resembles coarse crumbs. Make a well in the center of the dry ingredients. In a small mixing bowl combine egg, buttermilk or sour milk, and vanilla. Add all at once to dry ingredients. Stir *just till moistened*. ▼ **Spread batter** in prepared pan. Top with blueberries. Sprinkle Crumb Topping over blueberries. ▼ **Bake** in a 350° oven about 50 minutes or till a wooden toothpick inserted near center comes out clean. ▼ **Cool in pan** on a wire rack for 30 minutes. Invert onto a plate and remove waxed paper. Immediately invert the cake again onto a serving plate. Sprinkle with powdered sugar. Serve warm.

Crumb Topping

In a small mixing bowl stir together ¼ cup *all-purpose flour* and 2 tablespoons *sugar*. Cut in 2 tablespoons *margarine or butter* till mixture resembles coarse crumbs.

GOOSEBERRIES

Spiced Gooseberry Relish
Makes 1½ cups (24 one-tablespoon servings)

Gooseberries look like plump golden raisins in this sweet-and-sour, chutney-like sauce.

2 **cups gooseberries**
1 **cup packed brown sugar**
¼ **cup vinegar**
2 **tablespoons port wine** *or* **sweet marsala**
1 **teaspoon finely shredded orange peel**

▼
¼ **teaspoon ground cinnamon**
⅛ **teaspoon ground cloves**
⅛ **teaspoon ground allspice**
⅛ **teaspoon ground nutmeg**

Per Serving

Calories	42
Protein	0 g
Carbohydrate	11 g
Total Fat	0 g
Saturated Fat	0 g
Cholesterol	0 mg
Sodium	3 mg
Potassium	60 mg

Remove tops and stems from gooseberries; rinse and drain. In a 2-quart saucepan stir together berries, brown sugar, vinegar, wine, and orange peel. Bring to boiling; reduce heat. Simmer, uncovered, for 5 minutes, stirring frequently. ▼ **Stir cinnamon,** cloves, allspice, and nutmeg into the hot gooseberry mixture. Simmer, uncovered, for 5 minutes more, stirring often. Serve warm or chilled on ham, pork, or chicken. To store, cool to room temperature. Cover and chill for up to 2 weeks.

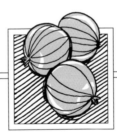

Some berries burst with flavor when eaten fresh; others taste better when cooked. The tart gooseberry, for most tastes, falls into the cooking category. People have created jams, jellies, pies, and meat

Goose-berries

sauces with these tiny, silvery-green berries for centuries. June and July are the peak of the domestic gooseberry season. If you find some, refrigerate them, loosely covered, for up to a week.

GOOSEBERRIES

Gingersnap-Gooseberry Pie

Makes 8 servings

Per Serving

Calories	470
Protein	5 g
Carbohydrate	69 g
Total Fat	20 g
Saturated Fat	5 g
Cholesterol	0 mg
Sodium	226 mg
Potassium	244 mg

**Pastry for Single-Crust Pie
(see recipe, page 163)**
▼
4 **cups gooseberries**
1¼ **cups sugar**
¼ **cup all-purpose flour**
¼ **teaspoon ground nutmeg**
¼ **cup apple juice**

1¼ **cups crushed gingersnaps
(about 18)**
½ **cup chopped almonds**
¼ **cup margarine *or* butter,
melted**
**Whipped cream
(optional)**

The almond and crushed gingersnap topping toasts as the pie bakes.

Prepare Pastry for Single-Crust Pie as directed. Line a 9-inch pie plate with the pastry. Trim and crimp the edge of the pastry. ▼ **For filling,** remove tops and stems from gooseberries; rinse and drain. In a medium mixing bowl stir together the sugar, flour, and nutmeg. Stir in gooseberries and apple juice. Spoon filling into the pastry shell. To prevent overbrowning, cover the edge of pie with foil. Bake in a 375° oven for 45 minutes. ▼ **Meanwhile,** in a small mixing bowl combine gingersnaps, almonds, and melted margarine or butter. Remove foil from pie. Top with almond mixture. Bake about 15 minutes more or till almonds are lightly toasted. Cool slightly on a wire rack. Serve warm with whipped cream, if desired.

Blackberry-Blueberry Cobbler Supreme

Makes 12 servings

If you've got frozen blackberries and blueberries, you can use them to make this fabulous cobbler. Just thaw the fruit, reserving the liquid. Then add enough grape juice or water to the fruit liquid to equal 2 cups. Use this liquid to pour over the fruit before baking the cobbler.

1 cup all-purpose flour
1 cup whole wheat flour
2 teaspoons baking powder
¼ teaspoon salt
½ cup margarine *or* butter, softened
1 cup sugar
¾ cup milk

▼
2 cups blackberries
1 cup blueberries
½ to ¾ cup sugar
2 cups grape juice *or* water
▼
Powdered sugar (optional)
Ice cream *or* light cream

Per Serving	
Calories	418
Protein	6 g
Carbohydrate	66 g
Total Fat	16 g
Saturated Fat	6 g
Cholesterol	31 mg
Sodium	257 mg
Potassium	321 mg

In a medium mixing bowl stir together all-purpose flour, whole wheat flour, baking powder, and salt. Beat margarine or butter and the 1 cup sugar with an electric mixer till fluffy. Add flour mixture alternately with milk. Beat till smooth. Spread batter evenly over the bottom of a greased 13x9x2-inch baking pan or a 3-quart baking dish. ▼ **Sprinkle blackberries** and blueberries over batter, then sprinkle with the ½ to ¾ cup sugar, depending on the sweetness of fruit. Pour grape juice or water over fruit. ▼ **Bake** in a 350° oven for 40 to 45 minutes or till a toothpick inserted in cake comes out clean. (Some of the fruit should sink toward the bottom as the cake rises to top.) Cool. Sprinkle lightly with powdered sugar, if desired. Serve warm with ice cream or cream.

Blackberry Swirl Cheesecake

Makes 12 to 16 servings

1 tablespoon margarine *or* butter, softened
2 cups finely chopped walnuts

▼

3 8-ounce packages cream cheese, softened
1 cup sugar
2 tablespoons all-purpose flour

1 teaspoon vanilla
2 eggs
1 egg yolk
¼ cup milk
½ teaspoon finely shredded orange peel

▼

Blackberry Sauce

Can't tell when your cheese-cakes are done? Well, if the cheesecake looks nearly set and only a small circle in the center jiggles slightly, it's done. The center will firm up during the cooling time.

Use softened margarine or butter to grease bottom and sides of an 8- or 9-inch springform pan. Press nuts onto bottom and about 2 inches up sides of an 8-inch springform pan or 1¾ inches up sides of a 9-inch springform pan. Set pan aside. ▼ **For filling,** in a large mixing bowl beat cream cheese, sugar, flour, and vanilla with an electric mixer on medium to high speed till combined. Add eggs and egg yolk all at once. Beat on low speed *just till combined.* Stir in milk and orange peel.

▼ **Pour half of filling** into crust-lined springform pan. Drizzle half of Blackberry Sauce atop. Repeat with remaining filling and Blackberry Sauce. Use a spatula to gently swirl the filling and Blackberry Sauce.

▼ **Bake cheesecake** on a shallow baking pan in a 375° oven for 50 to 55 minutes or till center of cheesecake appears nearly set. Cool cheesecake in springform pan on a wire rack for 15 minutes. Using a small metal spatula, loosen crust from the sides of the pan. Cool for 30 minutes more. Remove the sides of the springform pan. Cool the cheesecake completely, then chill for at least 4 hours.

Blackberry Sauce

In a medium saucepan combine 2 cups *blackberries,* 3 tablespoons *sugar,* 1 tablespoon *cornstarch,* and 1 tablespoon *water.* Cook and stir till thickened and bubbly. Cook and stir 2 minutes more. Press mixture through a fine sieve; discard seeds. Stir in 1 tablespoon *blackberry brandy or rum* and ½ teaspoon *finely shredded orange peel.* Cover and chill sauce.

RASPBERRIES

Raspberries, Honeydew, And Cream

Makes 4 servings

Cap berries and melon with this velvety, three-ingredient topping for a simply splendid summertime dessert. And for a different taste, next time try blueberries with cantaloupe.

½ **cup soft-style cream cheese**
½ **cup vanilla yogurt**
1 **tablespoon honey**

▼

1 **small honeydew melon, seeded, peeled, and cut into thin wedges**
2 **cups raspberries**

Per Serving

Calories	217
Protein	4 g
Carbohydrate	28 g
Total Fat	11 g
Saturated Fat	5 g
Cholesterol	32 mg
Sodium	132 mg
Potassium	483 mg

In a small bowl combine cream cheese, yogurt, and honey. Refrigerate, covered, till serving time. ▼ **To serve,** fan out honeydew wedges on 4 individual dessert plates. Stir cream cheese topping; spoon over melon. Top each serving with ½ cup of the raspberries. Refrigerate any leftover topping.

RASPBERRIES

Raspberry Ice

Makes 6 to 8 servings (3 cups)

The sweet flavor of the raspberries shines through in this refreshing dessert.

Per Serving

Calories	119
Protein	1 g
Carbohydrate	28 g
Total Fat	0 g
Saturated Fat	0 g
Cholesterol	0 mg
Sodium	1 mg
Potassium	157 mg

3 cups red raspberries
1 cup unsweetened white grape juice
½ cup sugar
2 tablespoons raspberry liqueur *or* orange liqueur

½ teaspoon finely shredded lemon peel *or* orange peel
Unsweetened white grape juice

In a blender container combine raspberries, white grape juice, sugar, raspberry liqueur or orange liqueur, and lemon peel or orange peel. Cover and blend till smooth. Press mixture through a sieve to remove seeds; discard. Add additional white grape juice, if necessary, to equal 3 cups mixture. ▼ **Transfer mixture** to an 8x4x2-inch or 9x5x3-inch loaf pan. Cover and freeze about 4 hours or till firm. Break the frozen mixture into small chunks. Transfer chunks to a chilled mixer bowl. Beat with an electric mixer on medium speed till smooth but not melted. Return quickly to the loaf pan. Cover and freeze till firm. ▼ **To serve,** scrape across top with spoon, mound into dessert dishes.

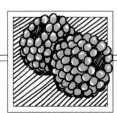

Storing Fresh Berries

When you get home from the farmer's market with your berries, refrigerate them in a single layer, loosely covered. Heaping the berries in a bowl or container will crush the delicate fruit and cause it to mold quickly. Use most of the berries within a couple of days.

Berries can be frozen by arranging washed berries, stems removed, on a baking sheet. Place in freezer until solid; transfer them to plastic freezer containers or bags, leaving ½-inch headspace. Return to freezer.

Raspberry-Hazelnut Meringue Torte

Makes 6 to 8 servings

What a spectacular way to end a meal!

4 egg whites
1 teaspoon vanilla
¼ teaspoon cream of tartar
¾ cup sugar
⅓ cup finely chopped hazel-nuts (filberts)

▼

1 cup whipping cream
1 tablespoon powdered sugar

▼

2 cups red *or* black raspberries
Fresh mint

Per Serving

Calories	325
Protein	5 g
Carbohydrate	33 g
Total Fat	21 g
Saturated Fat	10 g
Cholesterol	54 mg
Sodium	52 mg
Potassium	172 mg

Line one large or 2 medium baking sheets with parchment paper, plain brown paper, or foil. Draw three 7-inch circles, 1 inch apart, on the paper. Set baking sheet(s) aside. ▼ **In a large mixing bowl** beat egg whites, vanilla, and cream of tartar with an electric mixer on medium speed till soft peaks form (tips curl). Gradually add sugar, 1 tablespoon at a time, beating on high speed about 9 minutes or till very stiff peaks form (tips stand straight) and sugar is almost dissolved. Fold in hazelnuts. ▼ **Spread the meringue** mixture evenly over the three circles. Bake in a 300° oven for 20 minutes. Turn off the oven. Let the meringues dry in the oven with the door closed for 1 hour (do not open oven door). Meanwhile, in a medium mixing bowl beat whipping cream and powdered sugar till stiff peaks form. ▼ **To assemble torte,** peel meringue circles from paper. Place *one* meringue circle on a serving plate; spread *one-third* of the whipped cream on the meringue circle. Sprinkle ½ *cup* of the raspberries over the whipped cream. Repeat these layers once more. Place last meringue circle atop raspberries; spread with remaining whipped cream. Cover and chill for 4 to 6 hours. Just before serving, garnish top with remaining raspberries and mint.

Raspberry-Lemon Breakfast Biscuits

Makes 12

These drop biscuits are a cinch to make. Serve them warm with a cup of hot tea.

2 cups all-purpose flour
2 tablespoons sugar
1 tablespoon baking powder
1 tablespoon finely shredded lemon peel
½ teaspoon cream of tartar
¼ teaspoon salt

¼ teaspoon baking soda
½ cup margarine *or* butter
1 cup buttermilk *or* sour milk
1 cup red raspberries
▼
Lemon Butter Frosting

Per Serving

Calories	200
Protein	3 g
Carbohydrate	27 g
Total Fat	9 g
Saturated Fat	1 g
Cholesterol	1 mg
Sodium	265 mg
Potassium	79 mg

In a medium mixing bowl stir together flour, sugar, baking powder, lemon peel, cream of tartar, salt, and baking soda. Using a pastry blender, cut in margarine or butter till mixture resembles coarse crumbs. Make a well in center of dry ingredients; add buttermilk or sour milk all at once. Using a fork, stir *just till moistened*. Gently fold in raspberries. ▼ **Drop dough** from a tablespoon 1 inch apart on a greased baking sheet. Bake in a 450° oven for 10 to 12 minutes or till the biscuits are done. Remove biscuits from the baking sheet and let cool on a wire rack while preparing frosting. Frost tops of biscuits with Lemon Butter Frosting. Serve warm.

Lemon Butter Frosting

In a small mixing bowl stir together 1 cup sifted *powdered sugar* and 1 tablespoon softened *margarine or butter*. Stir in ¼ teaspoon finely shredded *lemon peel* and enough *water or lemon juice* to make of spreading consistency.

RASPBERRIES

Fresh Raspberry Mousse

Makes 4 servings

Per Serving

Calories	233
Protein	3 g
Carbohydrate	29 g
Total Fat	12 g
Saturated Fat	7 g
Cholesterol	41 mg
Sodium	15 mg
Potassium	208 mg

3 cups red raspberries
2 tablespoons raspberry liquer *or* white grape juice
▼
1 envelope unflavored gelatin

⅓ cup sugar
¾ cup boiling water
▼
½ cup whipping cream
▼
Raspberries (optional)
Fresh mint (optional)

Easy yet sophisticated—a great dessert for a summertime dinner party.

For raspberry puree, in a blender container or food processor bowl combine raspberries and raspberry liqueur or white grape juice. Cover and blend or process till smooth. Press mixture through a sieve to remove seeds; discard seeds. Set raspberry puree aside. ▼ **In a medium mixing bowl** combine gelatin and sugar; add the boiling water, stirring till gelatin dissolves. Stir in the raspberry puree. Transfer to a medium mixing bowl. Cover and chill till partially set (the consistency of unbeaten egg whites), stirring several times. ▼ **Beat the whipping cream** till soft peaks form. Fold whipped cream into partially set raspberry mixture. If necessary, chill again till the mixture mounds when spooned. Spoon into four wine glasses or dessert dishes. Cover and chill about 2 hours or till firm. ▼ **To serve,** garnish with raspberries and fresh mint, if desired.

Very Boysenberry Sorbet

Makes 4 servings (about 1 pint)

Boysenberries are a hybrid of blackberries, loganberries, and raspberries. They are a large, purplish-black berry with a sweet and tangy blackberry flavor and soft texture.

⅔ **cup water**
¼ **cup sugar**
1½ **cups boysenberries**

▼
½ **teaspoon finely shredded lemon peel**
1 **tablespoon lemon juice**

In a small saucepan combine the water and sugar. Bring to boiling; remove from heat. Cool; chill. Place the berries in a blender container or food processor bowl. Cover and blend or process till smooth. Press the berries through a sieve to remove seeds; discard seeds. ▼ **Combine the chilled** sugar mixture, sieved berries, lemon peel, and lemon juice; stir till well combined. Transfer mixture to an 8x4x2-inch loaf pan. Cover and freeze till almost firm. Break the frozen mixture into small chunks. Transfer chunks to a chilled mixer bowl. Beat with an electric mixer on medium speed till smooth but not melted. Return quickly to the cold pan. Cover and freeze till firm. ▼ **To serve,** let stand at room temperature for 5 minutes before serving.

Per Serving

Calories	71
Protein	1 g
Carbohydrate	18 g
Total Fat	0 g
Saturated Fat	0 g
Cholesterol	0 mg
Sodium	2 mg
Potassium	74 mg

VINEGARS

During the summer months, because of the abundance of fresh fruit and herbs, home-made vinegars pop up for sale at farmer's markets everywhere.

Fruit-flavored vinegars are not sweet, but have a fruity flavor that goes well with fruit salads and poultry and pork salads. Fruit vinegars are made with cider vinegar or white wine vinegar and any of a variety of fruits such as raspberries, strawberries, lemons, blueberries, or cranberries.

Herb-flavored vinegars are cider, white, or wine vinegars that have the added flavor of herbs such as basil, tarragon, oregano, thyme, mint, rosemary, dill, chervil, or garlic. These vinegars enhance the flavor of mild greens such as iceberg, butterhead, romaine, and leaf lettuce.

Fruit-Flavored Vinegar

Makes about 1½ cups (twenty-four 1-tablespoon servings)

Per Serving

Calories	6
Protein	0g
Carbohydrate	1g
Total Fat	0g
Saturated Fat	0g
Cholesterol	0g
Sodium	7mg
Potassium	21mg

1 cup pitted tart red cherries, blueberries, *or* raspberries

2 cups white wine vinegar

In a small stainless steel or enamel saucepan combine fruit and vinegar. Bring to boiling; reduce heat. Boil gently, uncovered, for 3 minutes. Remove from heat and cover loosely with cheesecloth; cool. Pour mixture into a clean 1-quart jar. Cover jar tightly with a nonmetallic lid (*or* cover with plastic wrap and then tightly seal with a metal lid). Let stand in a cool, dark place for 2 weeks. ▼ **Line a colander** with several layers of 100% cotton cheesecloth. Strain vinegar mixture through the colander and let it drain into a bowl. Discard fruit. Transfer strained vinegar to a clean 1-pint jar or bottle. If desired, add a few additional pieces of fresh fruit to the jar or bottle. Cover the jar or bottle tightly with a nonmetallic lid (*or* cover with plastic wrap and then seal tightly with a metal lid). Store vinegar in a cool, dark place for up to 6 months.

CRAB APPLES

Crab Apple Butter

Makes 5 half-pints (80 one-tablespoon servings)

Slather this spicy, rosy spread on your favorite breakfast bread or muffin.

3 **pounds crab apples**

▼

2½ **cups apple cider** *or* **apple juice**

½ **cup cider vinegar**

▼

2 **cups sugar**

1 **teaspoon ground cinnamon**

¼ **teaspoon ground nutmeg**

⅛ **teaspoon ground mace**

Per Serving

Calories	35
Protein	0 g
Carbohydrate	9 g
Total Fat	0 g
Saturated Fat	0 g
Cholesterol	0 mg
Sodium	0 mg
Potassium	44 mg

Rinse the crab apples; pat dry with paper towels. Core and quarter the crab apples. (You should have about 9 cups.) ▼ **In a large kettle** or Dutch oven combine the crab apples, apple cider or apple juice, and cider vinegar. Bring the mixture to boiling; reduce heat. Cover and simmer for 30 minutes, stirring occasionaly. ▼ **Press the mixture** through a food mill or sieve. Measure 5 cups of the pulp; return pulp to the kettle or Dutch oven. (Reserve the remaining pulp for another use such as applesauce.) ▼ **Stir the sugar,** cinnamon, nutmeg, and mace into the pulp in the kettle. Bring the mixture to boiling; reduce heat. Simmer, uncovered, for 1 to 1½ hours or till the mixture is very thick, stirring often. Spoon the hot mixture evenly into 5 hot, sterilized half-pint jars, leaving a ½-inch headspace. Adjust lids. Process in a boiling-water canner for 10 minutes. (Begin timing when water boils.)

To Freeze

Place kettle in a sink of *ice water* to cool apple butter. Spoon into freezer containers, leaving ½-inch headspace for pint containers and a 1-inch headspace for quart containers.

Apple Cake with Caramel-Raisin Sauce

Makes 12 servings

Per Serving

Calories	478
Protein	5 g
Carbohydrate	63 g
Total Fat	24 g
Saturated Fat	7 g
Cholesterol	58 mg
Sodium	349 mg
Potassium	243 mg

2 **cups all-purpose flour**
¾ **cup sugar**
½ **cup packed brown sugar**
2 **teaspoons baking powder**
1 **teaspoon ground cinnamon**
½ **teaspoon baking soda**
½ **teaspoon salt**
½ **teaspoon ground ginger**
¼ **teaspoon ground cloves**

▼

2 **slightly beaten eggs**
1 **8-ounce carton dairy sour cream**

¼ **cup margarine *or* butter, melted**
3 **tablespoons milk**
1 **teaspoon vanilla**
1 **medium apple, peeled and coarsely shredded (1 cup)**
⅔ **cup chopped walnuts**

▼

Caramel-Raisin Sauce

Grease and lightly flour an 8-inch springform pan or a 9x9x2-inch baking pan; set aside. ▼ **In a large mixing bowl** stir together the flour, sugar, brown sugar, baking powder, cinnamon, baking soda, salt, ginger, and cloves. Make a well in the center of the dry ingredients. ▼ **In a medium mixing bowl** combine eggs, sour cream, melted margarine or butter, milk, and vanilla. Add egg mixture all at once to dry ingredients. Stir *just till moistened.* Fold in shredded apple and nuts. Spread batter in the prepared pan. ▼ **Bake** in a 350° oven about 50 minutes for springform pan or about 45 minutes for 9x9x2-inch pan, or till a wooden toothpick inserted near center comes out clean. Cool in pan on a wire rack for 20 minutes. Remove sides of the springform pan (can remove or leave cake in the 9x9x2-inch pan). Serve warm or cool with Caramel-Raisin Sauce.

Caramel-Raisin Sauce

In a medium saucepan melt ½ cup *margarine or butter.* Stir in 1 cup packed *brown sugar* and 2 tablespoons *light corn syrup.* Cook and stir over medium heat until mixture comes to a full boil. Stir in ½ cup *whipping cream.* Return to a full boil. Remove from heat and stir in ¼ cup *raisins.* Serve warm. Makes about 2 cups.

Deep Dish Apple Pie

Makes 8 servings

Hate slicing apples for apple pie? You only have to quarter the apples for this country dessert.

3 cups apple cider *or* apple juice

▼

10 medium cooking apples, peeled, cored, and quartered

▼

½ cup sugar
½ cup raisins
3 tablespoons all-purpose flour
½ teaspoon ground cinnamon

¼ teaspoon ground nutmeg
¼ teaspoon ground cardamom
1 tablespoon margarine *or* butter

▼

Whole Wheat Pastry
1 tablespoon milk
1 to 2 tablespoons sugar

▼

Rum-Cider Sauce
Ice cream (optional)

Per Serving

Calories	539
Protein	4 g
Carbohydrate	87 g
Total Fat	21 g
Saturated Fat	5 g
Cholesterol	0 mg
Sodium	175 mg
Potassium	463 mg

Simmer cider 20 minutes or till reduced to 1¾ cups. Remove ¼ cup; reserve remaining for Rum-Cider Sauce. ▼ **Simmer apples** and ¼ cup reduced cider, covered, 5 to 6 minutes or till apples are barely tender. ▼ **Mix** ½ cup sugar, raisins, flour, and spices. Stir into apple mixture; transfer to a 12x7½x2-inch baking dish. Dot with margarine ▼ **Prepare Pastry.** On a floured surface, roll dough into a 13x9-inch rectangle; place atop fruit. Trim pastry ½ inch beyond edge of dish. Fold under extra pastry; crimp edge to sides of dish. Cut several 2- to 3-inch slits into pastry. Brush with milk; sprinkle with the 1 to 2 tablespoons sugar. ▼ **Cover** edge of pie with foil; place on a baking sheet. Bake in a 375° oven 25 minutes. Remove foil. Bake 20 to 25 minutes more or till golden. Serve warm with sauce and ice cream, if desired.

Whole Wheat Pastry
Combine 1 cup *all-purpose flour,* ¾ cup *whole wheat flour,* and ¼ teaspoon *salt.* Cut in ½ cup *shortening or lard* till pieces are the size of small peas. Sprinkle 5 to 6 tablespoons *cold water,* 1 tablespoon at a time, over mixture, tossing with a fork after each addition. Form dough into a ball.

Rum-Cider Sauce
Melt ¼ cup *margarine or butter.* Stir in reserved *reduced cider,* ⅓ cup packed *brown sugar,* 2 tablespoons *dark rum,* 4 teaspoons *cornstarch,* ⅛ teaspoon *ground cinnamon,* and a dash each of *ground nutmeg* and *cardamom,* and *salt.* Cook and stir till bubbly. Cook 2 minutes more.

Home-Style Baked Apple Wedges

Makes 6 to 8 servings

This cakelike dessert with apples, raisins, and pecans mixes up by hand in just minutes.

1 tablespoon margarine *or* butter, softened
1 cup all-purpose flour
2 teaspoons baking powder
¼ teaspoon salt
2 eggs
1 cup sugar

2 medium cooking apples, peeled and finely chopped (2 cups)
½ cup chopped pecans, toasted
2 tablespoons raisins

▼

Whipped cream (optional)

Per Serving

Calories	322
Protein	5 g
Carbohydrate	56 g
Total Fat	10 g
Saturated Fat	1 g
Cholesterol	71 mg
Sodium	243 mg
Potassium	134 mg

Generously grease a 9-inch pie plate with the 1 tablespoon margarine or butter; set aside. In a small bowl combine flour, baking powder, and salt. In a large mixing bowl beat eggs by hand till foamy. Stir in sugar. Add flour mixture, stirring till well combined (mixture will be stiff). Stir in apples, pecans, and raisins. Spread evenly in prepared pie plate.

▼ **Bake** in a 325° oven about 50 minutes or till golden brown and center appears set. Serve warm with whipped cream, if desired.

Apple-Cherry Cobbler

Makes 4 servings

Per Serving

Calories	286
Protein	5 g
Carbohydrate	48 g
Total Fat	9 g
Saturated Fat	3 g
Cholesterol	59 mg
Sodium	129 mg
Potassium	178 mg

⅔ **cup all-purpose flour**
2 **tablespoons whole wheat flour** *or* **all-purpose flour**
2 **tablespoons sugar**
½ **teaspoon baking powder**
2 **tablespoons margarine** *or* **butter**
1 **egg**
1 **tablespoon milk**
   ▼
2 **medium cooking apples, peeled, cored, and thinly sliced (2 cups)**

1½ **cups pitted tart red cherries**
¼ **cup sugar**
2 **tablespoons water**
1 **tablespoon cornstarch**
   ▼
1 **teaspoon sugar**
¼ **teaspoon ground cinnamon**
   ▼
¼ **cup half-and-half** *or* **light cream (optional)**

What apple variety works best in baked recipes? Look for Golden Delicious, Granny Smith, or Jonathan apples.

For biscuit topping, in a medium mixing bowl combine flour, whole wheat flour, the 2 tablespoons sugar, and baking powder. Cut in margarine or butter till mixture resembles coarse crumbs. Combine egg and milk; set aside. ▼ **For filling,** in a medium saucepan combine apples, cherries, the ¼ cup sugar, and *1 tablespoon* of the water. Bring to boiling; reduce heat. Cover and simmer for 5 minutes or till apples are almost tender, stirring occasionally. Combine cornstarch with the remaining water; add to fruit. Cook and stir over medium heat till thickened and bubbly. Transfer hot filling to a 1-quart casserole. Place on a baking sheet to catch any spills. ▼ **Add the egg-milk mixture** all at once to the dry ingredients, stirring just till moistened. Immediately spoon topping into 4 mounds atop hot filling. Stir together the 1 teaspoon sugar and cinnamon; sprinkle over dough. ▼ **Bake** in a 400° oven about 15 minutes or till a toothpick inserted into topping comes out clean. Serve warm with half-and-half or light cream, if desired.

Sherried Pears

Makes 6 servings

A cozy dessert for a crisp, fall evening.

3 medium pears

▼

⅓ cup packed brown sugar
¼ cup water
¼ cup cream sherry *or* port
1 tablespoon margarine *or* butter, cut up

1 tablespoon lemon juice
½ teaspoon ground cinnamon

▼

Vanilla ice cream (optional)

Per Serving

Calories	128
Protein	0 g
Carbohydrate	26 g
Total Fat	2 g
Saturated Fat	0 g
Cholesterol	0 mg
Sodium	27 mg
Potassium	158 mg

Halve pears lengthwise; remove cores. To fan pears, place halves, cut side down, on a cutting board. With a sharp, fine-bladed knife, make lengthwise cuts from blossom end of pear to, but not through, stem end. Fan out each pear half. Place pears, cut side down, in an 8x8x2-inch baking dish. ▼ **In a small saucepan** combine brown sugar, water, sherry or port, margarine or butter, lemon juice, and cinnamon. Cook and stir over medium heat till heated through; pour over pears. ▼ **Bake,** covered, in a 350° oven for 35 to 40 minutes or till tender, spooning sauce over pears occasionally. Serve warm with ice cream, if desired.

Honey-Pear Ice

Makes 12 servings (about 1½ quarts)

Per Serving

Calories	107
Protein	2 g
Carbohydrate	26 g
Total Fat	0 g
Saturated Fat	0 g
Cholesterol	2 mg
Sodium	45 mg
Potassium	103 mg

1 envelope unflavored gelatin
½ cup sugar
¼ cup cold water
▼
1 medium pear, peeled and chopped (1 cup)

½ cup pear, apricot, *or* peach nectar
2 cups buttermilk
½ cup honey
1 teaspoon vanilla

A refreshing, creamy blend of fruit and buttermilk.

In a small saucepan combine gelatin and sugar; stir in water. Cook and stir over medium heat till gelatin dissolves. ▼ **In a blender** container combine chopped pear and the nectar. Cover and blend till smooth. Combine gelatin mixture, pear mixture, buttermilk, honey, and vanilla. Transfer to an 8x8x2-inch pan. Cover and freeze about 4 hours or till firm. Break frozen mixture into small chunks. Transfer to a chilled mixer bowl. Beat with electric mixer on medium speed till smooth but not melted. Return quickly to cold pan. Cover and freeze till firm.

Chicken and Pear Stir-Fry

Makes 4 servings

4 **medium boneless, skin-less chicken breast halves (12 ounces)** *or* **12 ounces turkey breast-tenderloin steaks**

▼

⅔ **cup pear nectar** *or* **orange juice**
2 **tablespoons soy sauce**
1 **tablespoon cornstarch**
⅛ **teaspoon ground red pepper**

▼

1 **tablespoon cooking oil**
1 **teaspoon grated gingerroot**

1 **medium green, yellow,** *or* **red sweet pepper, cut into ¾-inch pieces (1 cup)**
1 **medium leek, thinly sliced (⅓ cup)** *or* **3 green onions, thinly sliced (6 tablespoons)**
¼ **cup broken pecans**

▼

2 **medium pears, cored, cut into eight slices, and halved crosswise (2 cups)**
3 **cups hot cooked brown rice**

Per Serving

Calories	434
Protein	21 g
Carbohydrate	62 g
Total Fat	12 g
Saturated Fat	2 g
Cholesterol	45 mg
Sodium	563 mg
Potassium	470 mg

Rinse chicken or turkey and pat dry. Cut into thin, bite-size strips. Set aside. ▼ **For sauce,** stir together the pear nectar or orange juice, soy sauce, cornstarch, and ground red pepper. Set sauce aside. ▼ **Pour cooking oil** into a wok or a large skillet. (Add more oil as necessary during cooking.) Preheat over medium-high heat. Stir-fry gingerroot in hot oil for 15 seconds. Add sweet pepper and leek or green onion. Stir-fry 1½ to 2 minutes or till vegetables are crisp-tender. Remove the vegetables from the wok. Add the pecans. Stir-fry about 1 minute or till toasted. Remove pecans from wok. ▼ **Add the chicken** to the hot wok. Stir-fry for 2 to 3 minutes or till no pink remains. Push the chicken from center of wok. Stir sauce, add to the center of the wok. Cook and stir till thickened and bubbly. ▼ **Return the cooked vegetables** to the wok. Add the pears. Stir all the ingredients together to coat with the sauce. Cook and stir about 1 minute more or till heated through. Serve immediately over brown rice. Sprinkle with the toasted pecans.

Pears and Puff Pastry With Chocolate Sauce

Makes 8 servings

Once ripened, you can keep fresh pears in the refrigerator for several days.

Per Serving

Calories	499
Protein	4 g
Carbohydrate	64 g
Total Fat	26 g
Saturated Fat	1 g
Cholesterol	5 mg
Sodium	288 mg
Potassium	216 mg

1 17½-ounce package (2 sheets) frozen puff pastry

▼

4 medium pears
¾ cup water
⅓ cup sugar
½ teaspoon finely shredded orange peel

¼ cup sweet white wine *or* orange juice
⅛ teaspoon ground nutmeg

▼

Chocolate Sauce
Orange peel twists (optional)

To thaw puff pastry, let stand at room temperature 20 minutes. Or, thaw overnight in the refrigerator. ▼ **Line a** 15x10x1-inch baking pan with parchment or plain brown paper. Set aside. Unfold pastry; place on a lightly floured surface. Roll each sheet to a 10-inch square. Cut pastry into eight 4½- to 5-inch circles. Place pastry circles on prepared baking pan. Place a second baking pan atop pastry circles to keep them flat. Bake in a 400° oven 15 to 20 minutes or till golden. Remove rounds from baking pan. Cool. ▼ **Meanwhile,** peel pears, if desired. Halve pears lengthwise; remove cores. In a large skillet bring water, sugar, orange peel, sweet white wine or orange juice, and nutmeg to boiling. Add pear halves. Reduce heat. Simmer, covered, 10 to 15 minutes or till pears are tender. Cool pears slightly in cooking liquid. ▼ **To serve,** spoon a little of the Chocolate Sauce onto 8 dessert plates; place a puff pastry round on each dessert plate. To fan pears, place halves, cut side down, on a cutting board. With a sharp, fine-bladed knife, make length-wise cuts from blossom end of pear to, but not through, stem ends. Fan out each pear half. Place each pear fan on top of a puff pastry round. Drizzle remaining Chocolate Sauce over pear and puff pastry. Garnish with orange peel twists, if desired.

Chocolate Sauce

In a small saucepan melt ½ cup *semisweet chocolate pieces* and 2 table-spoons *margarine or butter*. Add ½ cup *sugar*; gradually stir in ½ cup *evaporated milk* and ½ teaspoon *finely shredded orange peel*. Boil gently over low heat for 8 minutes, stirring frequently. Makes 1 cup.

Brandied Custard Pears

Makes 4 servings

To prevent a rubbery film from forming on this elegant custard, make sure the plastic wrap is pressed onto the surface of the custard while it's chilling.

2 beaten eggs
¾ cup half-and-half, light cream, *or* milk
2 tablespoons sugar
1 tablespoon brandy
▼
2 medium pears, sliced (2 cups)

1 tablespoon margarine *or* butter
▼
4 1-inch slices pound cake
¼ cup broken pecans, toasted

Per Serving

Calories	382
Protein	7 g
Carbohydrate	37 g
Total Fat	23 g
Saturated Fat	11 g
Cholesterol	197 mg
Sodium	147 mg
Potassium	234 mg

For custard, in a heavy medium saucepan combine eggs, half-and-half, light cream, or milk, and sugar. Cook and stir over medium heat. Continue cooking egg mixture till it just coats a metal spoon. Remove from the heat. Quickly add brandy, and cool custard by placing the saucepan in a sink or bowl of *ice water* for 1 to 2 minutes, stirring constantly. Pour custard mixture into a small mixing bowl. Cover surface with plastic wrap and chill till serving time. ▼ **In a medium skillet** cook pear slices, covered, in margarine or butter over medium-low heat for 4 minutes; uncover and cook for 2 to 3 minutes more or till just tender. Remove pear slices with a slotted spoon. ▼ **To serve,** place one slice of pound cake on each of four dessert plates. Spoon one-fourth of the cooked pear slices atop each cake slice. Top each serving with one-fourth of the custard. Sprinkle each serving with pecans.

CRANBERRIES

Cranberry-Pecan Pound Cake

Makes 16 to 20 servings

Per Serving

Calories	396
Protein	5 g
Carbohydrate	54 g
Total Fat	18 g
Saturated Fat	8 g
Cholesterol	86 mg
Sodium	180 mg
Potassium	81 mg

1 cup butter (do not use margarine)
4 eggs
¼ cup dairy sour cream
▼
3 cups all-purpose flour
1 teaspoon baking powder
½ teaspoon baking soda
¼ teaspoon ground nutmeg

▼
2 cups sugar
¼ cup orange liqueur *or* orange juice
1 teaspoon vanilla
1½ cups chopped cranberries
1 cup chopped pecans
▼
Orange Drizzle Icing

Because of the density of this sour cream pound cake batter, our test kitchen recommends using a sturdy, free-standing electric mixer, not a portable electric mixer.

Bring butter, eggs, and sour cream to room temperature (do not allow eggs to sit at room temperature longer than 30 minutes). Grease and lightly flour a 10-inch tube pan; set aside. ▼ **In a medium mixing** bowl stir together flour, baking powder, baking soda, and nutmeg. ▼ **In a large mixer bowl** beat butter with an electric freestanding mixer on medium to high speed about 30 seconds or till softened. Gradually add sugar, 2 tablespoons at a time, beating on medium to high speed about 8 minutes total or till very light and fluffy. Add orange liqueur or orange juice and vanilla. Add eggs, one at a time, beating on low to medium speed for 1 minute after adding each egg, and scraping the bowl often. Alternately add flour mixture and sour cream, beating on low speed *just till combined.* Fold in cranberries and pecans. ▼ **Spread batter** in the prepared pan. Bake in a 325° oven for 1 to 1¼ hours or till a toothpick inserted near the center comes out clean. Cool cake in pan on a wire rack for 10 minutes. Remove cake from pan and cool completely. Drizzle Orange Drizzle Icing over cooled cake.

Orange Drizzle Icing

In a small mixing bowl combine 1½ cups sifted *powdered sugar,* ½ teaspoon finely shredded *orange peel,* 1 tablespoon *orange liqueur or orange juice,* and enough *water or additional orange juice* (3 to 4 teaspoons) to make icing of drizzling consistency.

CRANBERRIES

Cranberry-Cornmeal Muffins

Makes 12

Per Serving

Calories	174
Protein	3 g
Carbohydrate	24 g
Total Fat	7 g
Saturated Fat	1 g
Cholesterol	18 mg
Sodium	121 mg
Potassium	72 mg

Something a little bit different for Thanksgiving dinner.

1 cup all-purpose flour
¾ cup cornmeal
⅓ cup sugar
2 teaspoons baking powder
¼ teaspoon salt
▼
1 beaten egg
¾ cup buttermilk

¼ cup cooking oil
½ teaspoon finely shredded lemon peel
1 cup coarsely chopped cranberries
2 tablespoons sugar
¼ cup finely chopped walnuts

Grease twelve 2½-inch muffin cups or line with paper bake cups. Set muffin cups aside. ▼ **In a medium mixing bowl** combine flour, cornmeal, the ⅓ cup sugar, baking powder, and salt. Make a well in the center of the dry ingredients. ▼ **In a small mixing bowl** combine egg, buttermilk, cooking oil, and lemon peel. Add egg mixture all at once to dry ingredients. Stir *just till moistened* (batter should be lumpy). In another small mixing bowl combine cranberries and the 2 tablespoons sugar. Fold cranberries and walnuts into muffin batter. Spoon batter into prepared muffin cups, filling each ⅔ full. ▼ **Bake** in a 400° oven about 20 minutes or till golden. Remove muffins from muffin cups. Cool slightly on a wire rack. Serve warm.

CRANBERRIES

Cranberry-Pear Conserve

Makes about 6 half-pints (96 one-tablespoon servings)

A conserve is a jam-like spread that usually includes raisins and/or nuts. This lush spread takes advantage of abundant fall fruit— cranberries and pears.

4 **cups cranberries**
4 **medium fully ripe pears, peeled and chopped (4 cups)**
2 **teaspoons finely shredded orange peel**
¼ **cup orange juice**
6 **cups sugar**
½ **cup broken walnuts**

Per Serving

Calories	56
Protein	0 g
Carbohydrate	14 g
Total Fat	0 g
Saturated Fat	0 g
Cholesterol	0 mg
Sodium	0 mg
Potassium	16 mg

In a 6- to 8-quart kettle or Dutch oven combine cranberries, pears, orange peel, and orange juice. Bring to boiling over medium heat, stirring occasionally. Continue to cook over medium heat for 5 minutes. Stir in sugar and nuts. Cook for 15 to 20 minutes more or till thickened. As mixture thickens, stir frequently and carefully to prevent sticking.

▼ **Ladle** mixture at once into hot, sterilized half-pint jars, leaving a ¼-inch headspace. (Use a canning funnel to avoid getting mixture on sides of jars.) Adjust lids. Process in a boiling-water canner for 15 minutes. (Begin timing when water boils.)

GRAPES

Spiced Grape Jelly

Makes 7 half-pints (112 one-tablespoon servings)

Per Serving

Calories	54
Protein	0 g
Carbohydrate	14 g
Total Fat	0 g
Saturated Fat	0 g
Cholesterol	0 mg
Sodium	1 mg
Potassium	26 mg

3 **pounds Concord grapes**
½ **cup water**
6 **inches stick cinnamon, broken**
6 **whole cloves**
3 **cardamom pods, opened**
1 **teaspoon finely shredded lemon peel**

▼

7 **cups sugar**
1 **6-ounce package (2 foil pouches) liquid fruit pectin**

Cinnamon, cloves, and cardamom are what "spice up" this wonderful fall treat.

Wash and stem grapes. Crush grapes, 2 cups at a time. In a saucepan bring grapes, water, cinnamon, cloves, cardamom, and lemon peel to boiling; reduce heat Cover; simmer 10 minutes. Strain mixture through a jelly bag or 100% cotton cheesecloth. Measure 4 cups juice (if necessary, add water to equal 4 cups). ▼ **In an 8- to 10-quart kettle** mix juice and sugar. Bring to a full rolling boil, stirring constantly. Stir in pectin. Return to full rolling boil; boil hard 1 minute, stirring constantly. Remove from heat; quickly skim off foam. ▼ **Ladle** into hot, sterilized half-pint jars, leaving a ¼-inch headspace. Adjust lids. Process in a boiling-water canner 5 minutes. (Begin timing when water boils.)

Concord Grapes

Did you know that the Concord grape is one of the few fruits native to North America? These large, purplish-blue grapes were introduced to the world in 1854 by Ephraim Wales Bull of (where else?) Concord, Massachusetts. Bull spent 20 years experimenting with the wild grapes that grew behind his house before winning first prize at a horticultural show for his vines.

The season for Concord grapes is short—just a couple of months in early fall—and they grow mainly in the Northeast. Today, Concords are most widely used for jams, jellies, and juice.

GRAPES

Concord Grape Pie

Makes 8 servings

If you close your eyes, you'll think you're eating grape jelly!

6 cups Concord grapes

▼

¾ cup sugar
¼ cup all-purpose flour
1 ¼ teaspoons finely shredded
    lemon peel (optional)
1 beaten egg yolk
2 tablespoons margarine *or*
    butter, cut up

▼

Pastry for Double-Crust
    Pie (see recipe,
    page 149)

▼

1 beaten egg white
1 tablespoon sugar

Per Serving

Calories	444
Protein	5 g
Carbohydrate	62 g
Total Fat	21 g
Saturated Fat	5 g
Cholesterol	27 mg
Sodium	177 mg
Potassium	247 mg

For filling, slip skins from grapes; set aside both grapes and skins. In a medium saucepan bring grape pulp to boiling. Reduce heat and simmer, covered, for 5 minutes. Sieve to remove seeds. ▼ **In a medium mixing bowl** combine grape skins, the ¾ cup sugar, flour, egg yolk, and margarine or butter. Stir in sieved grape pulp. Set filling aside. ▼ **Prepare and roll** out Pastry for Double-Crust Pie as directed. Line a 9-inch pie plate with half of the pastry. Stir filling; transfer to the pastry-lined pie plate. Trim the bottom pastry to edge of pie plate. Cut slits in the top crust. Place top crust on filling. Trim top crust ½ inch beyond edge of plate. Fold top crust under bottom pastry. Seal and crimp edge of pastry. ▼ **To prevent overbrowning,** cover edge of pie with foil. Bake in a 375° oven for 25 minutes. Remove foil. Bake for 20 minutes more or till filling is set. Combine egg white and the 1 tablespoon sugar; brush over crust. Return to oven and bake about 5 minutes more or till top is golden. Cool pie on a wire rack.

GRAPES

Grape-Bulgur Salad

Makes 4 to 6 servings

¾ **cup bulgur**
1 **cup halved seedless green**
  or red grapes
¼ **cup sliced radishes**
2 **green onions, thinly**
  sliced (¼ cup)

▼
⅓ **cup lemon juice**
¼ **cup salad oil**
1 **tablespoon water**
¼ **teaspoon salt**
⅛ **teaspoon pepper**
1½ **cups shredded red-tipped**
  leaf lettuce *or* spinach

When you bring your grapes home, refrigerate them in plastic bags for up to a week. Don't wash them till just before serving.

Rinse bulgur in a colander with cold water; drain. In a medium mixing bowl combine bulgur, grapes, radishes, and green onion.
▼ **For dressing,** in a screw-top jar combine lemon juice, salad oil, water, salt, and pepper. Cover and shake well. Pour dressing over bulgur mixture. Toss lightly to coat. Cover and chill for 4 to 24 hours. Before serving, stir in shredded lettuce or spinach.

Harvest Squash and Apple Soup

Makes 4 to 6 servings

Purée acorn squash with apple cider and top with sour cream for this exquisite first-course soup.

1 **medium onion, chopped (½ cup)**

1 **small carrot, sliced (⅓ cup)**

1¾ **cups apple cider** *or* **apple juice**

1 **teaspoon instant chicken bouillon granules**

1 **teaspoon lemon juice**

¼ **teaspoon ground ginger**

¼ **teaspoon white pepper**

▼

2 **cups cooked, mashed acorn squash**

1 **cup milk, half-and-half,** *or* **light cream**

▼

Dairy sour cream (optional)

Snipped fresh chives (optional)

Per Serving

Calories	163
Protein	4 g
Carbohydrate	36 g
Total Fat	2 g
Saturated Fat	1 g
Cholesterol	5 mg
Sodium	267 mg
Potassium	771 mg

In a large saucepan cook onion and carrot in apple cider or apple juice, covered, for 12 minutes or till very tender. *Do not drain.* Stir in bouillon granules, lemon juice, ginger, and pepper. ▼ **Transfer** to a blender container or food processor bowl. Add mashed squash. Cover and blend or process till smooth. Return squash mixture to saucepan. Stir in milk, half-and-half, or light cream. Bring to boiling, stirring constantly. Reduce heat; cover and simmer for 5 to 10 minutes or till flavors are blended, stirring once or twice. ▼ **Top each serving** with sour cream, if desired. Garnish with snipped chives, if desired.

SQUASH

Honey-Butternut Stir-Fry

Makes 4 servings

Per Serving

Calories	152
Protein	3 g
Carbohydrate	16 g
Total Fat	10 g
Saturated Fat	1 g
Cholesterol	0 mg
Sodium	22 mg
Potassium	404 mg

1 **pound butternut squash**
▼
2 **tablespoons cooking oil**
1 **teaspoon toasted sesame oil**
1 **clove garlic, minced**
½ **teaspoon grated ginger-root**
1 **cup broccoli flowerets**

½ **cup bias-sliced celery**
½ **of a small onion, thinly sliced and separated into rings**
1 **tablespoon lemon juice**
2 **teaspoons honey**
2 **tablespoons shelled sunflower seeds**

This is a colorful side dish that goes together in a hurry.

Peel, seed, and slice squash into ¼-inch thick slices. Cut slices into small pie-shaped wedges. (You should have about 2 cups.) ▼ **Pour cooking oil** and sesame oil into a large skillet or wok. (Add more oil as necessary during cooking.) Preheat over medium-high heat. Stir-fry the squash, garlic, and gingerroot in hot oil for 3 minutes. Add broccoli, celery, and onion. Stir-fry for 3 to 4 minutes more or till vegetables are crisp-tender. Combine lemon juice and honey; toss with vegetables. Top with sunflower seeds.

Twice-Baked Squash

Makes 4 servings

Per Serving

Calories	241
Protein	9 g
Carbohydrate	23 g
Total Fat	14 g
Saturated Fat	4 g
Cholesterol	12 mg
Sodium	479 mg
Potassium	846 mg

2 **medium acorn squash**

▼

1¼ **cups chopped cooked spinach** *or* **one 10-ounce package frozen chopped spinach, thawed and well drained**

⅓ **cup grated Parmesan** *or* **Romano cheese**

3 **slices bacon, crisp-cooked, drained, and crumbled**

3 **tablespoons margarine** *or* **butter, softened**

1 **green onion, thinly sliced (2 tablespoons)**

⅛ **teaspoon salt**

⅛ **teaspoon ground red pepper**

2 **tablespoons soft bread crumbs**

1 **tablespoon grated Parmesan** *or* **Romano cheese**

Serve these spinach-filled acorn squash with roast pork.

Halve squash lengthwise. Remove seeds. Place squash, cut side down, in a large baking dish. Bake in a 350° oven for 30 minutes. Turn cut side up. Bake, covered, for 20 to 25 minutes or till nearly tender. ▼ **Scoop out** squash pulp to make ¼-inch-thick shells. In a large mixing bowl combine squash pulp, spinach, the ⅓ cup Parmesan or Romano cheese, bacon, margarine or butter, green onion, salt, and red pepper. Fill the squash shells with the squash mixture. Combine the bread crumbs and the 1 tablespoon Parmesan or Romano cheese; sprinkle over squash. ▼ **Return** filled squash halves to same baking dish. Bake, uncovered, for 25 to 30 minutes or till heated through.

TURNIPS

Turnips in Thyme Dressing

Makes 4 servings

Use a sweet onion, such as a Vidalia or Maui, in this chilled vegetable dish.

½ **pound turnips (3 medium)**
1 **large carrot, thinly sliced (1 cup)**
▼
¼ **cup dairy sour cream** *or* **plain yogurt**
2 **tablespoons mayonnaise** *or* **salad dressing**

1 **tablespoon snipped fresh thyme** *or* ½ **teaspoon dried thyme, crushed**
2 **teaspoons Dijon-style mustard**
1 **to 2 tablespoons milk**
▼
1 **medium onion, thinly sliced**

Per Serving

Calories	124
Protein	2 g
Carbohydrate	11 g
Total Fat	9 g
Saturated Fat	3 g
Cholesterol	11 mg
Sodium	172 mg
Potassium	299 mg

Wash and peel the turnips; cut into ¾-inch cubes. (You should have about 2 cups.) Cook turnips, covered, in a small amount of boiling salted water for 5 minutes. Add the carrot and cook for 5 to 7 minutes more or till tender. Drain well. ▼ **Meanwhile,** for dressing, in a medium mixing bowl stir together sour cream or yogurt, mayonnaise or salad dressing, thyme, and mustard. Stir in the milk to make the dressing the desired consistency. ▼ **Gently stir** the cooked turnips, carrots, and onion into the dressing. Cover and chill for 4 to 24 hours. If necessary, stir in enough additional milk to moisten.

TURNIPS

Turnip Cakes With Apple

Makes 4 servings (2 to 3 cakes per serving)

Per Serving

Calories	140
Protein	3 g
Carbohydrate	14 g
Total Fat	8 g
Saturated Fat	1 g
Cholesterol	53 mg
Sodium	172 mg
Potassium	182 mg

1 **pound turnips (3 medium)**
1 **small baking potato**
▼
3 **tablespoons all-purpose flour**
1 **slightly beaten egg**
1 **small cooking apple, peeled, cored, and chopped (¾ cup)**

1 **tablespoon fresh snipped tarragon *or* ¼ teaspoon dried tarragon, crushed**
¼ **teaspoon salt**
▼
2 **tablespoons cooking oil**

Keep turnips refrigerated in a plastic bag for up to a week.

Wash and peel turnips and potato. Finely shred the turnips and the potato into a bowl of water. Drain well, squeezing out water. Squeeze the shredded vegetables in paper towels to remove any excess liquid. ▼ **In a large mixing bowl** toss the shredded vegetables with the flour. Stir in the egg, apple, tarragon, and salt. ▼ **In a large heavy skillet** heat cooking oil (add more cooking oil as necessary during cooking). Drop rounded tablespoons of the vegetable mixture into hot cooking oil. Flatten mounds with a slotted spatula. Cook for 3 minutes or till golden, turning once. Drain on paper towels. ▼ **Place turnip cakes** on a baking sheet and keep warm in a 300° oven while frying remaining cakes.

TURNIPS

Turnip and Cheddar Soufflé

Makes 4 servings

No chives on hand? Snip the tops of some green onions instead.

3 tablespoons margarine *or* butter
¼ cup all-purpose flour
¼ teaspoon salt
¼ teaspoon ground nutmeg
⅛ teaspoon pepper
1 cup milk
1 cup shredded sharp cheddar cheese (4 ounces)

1 cup finely chopped cooked turnip
2 tablespoons snipped fresh chives
▼
3 egg yolks
▼
3 egg whites
▼
Snipped fresh chives (optional)

Per Serving

Calories	312
Protein	15 g
Carbohydrate	11 g
Total Fat	23 g
Saturated Fat	9 g
Cholesterol	194 mg
Sodium	505 mg
Potassium	241 mg

In a medium saucepan melt margarine or butter. Stir in the flour, salt, nutmeg, and pepper. Add milk all at once. Cook and stir till thickened and bubbly. Remove from heat. Add shredded cheese and stir till melted. Stir in cooked turnips and chives. ▼ **In a large mixing bowl** beat egg yolks with a fork till combined. Gradually add turnip mixture, stirring constantly. Set aside. ▼ **In a medium mixing bowl** beat egg whites till stiff peaks form (tips stand straight). Gently fold about 1 cup of the beaten egg whites into the turnip mixture to lighten it. Gradually pour turnip mixture over remaining beaten egg whites, folding to combine. Pour into an ungreased 1½-quart soufflé dish or 1½-quart casserole. ▼ **Bake** in a 350° oven about 40 minutes or till a knife inserted near the center comes out clean. Garnish with additional chives, if desired. Serve immediately.

SWEET POTATOES

Sweet Potato Pie with Hazelnut Streusel Topper

Makes 8 servings

Sweet potato pie is not as sweet as pumpkin pie, but has a similar appearance.

Per Serving

Calories	456
Protein	7 g
Carbohydrate	52 g
Total Fat	25 g
Saturated Fat	6 g
Cholesterol	91 mg
Sodium	214 mg
Potassium	341 mg

1 pound sweet potatoes
¼ cup margarine *or* butter

▼

Cornmeal Pastry

▼

½ cup packed brown sugar
1 tablespoon finely shredded orange peel

1 teaspoon ground cinnamon
½ teaspoon ground nutmeg
½ teaspoon ground ginger
3 slightly beaten eggs
1 cup half-and-half

▼

Hazelnut Streusel Topper

Peel sweet potatoes. Cut off woody portions and ends. Cut into quarters. Cook, covered, in enough boiling salted water to cover for 25 to 35 minutes or till tender; mash. (You should have 1½ cups.) Cut up margarine or butter; add to hot potatoes, stirring till melted. ▼ **Meanwhile,** prepare Cornmeal Pastry. Roll dough into a 12-inch circle; ease into a 9-inch pie plate. Trim pastry to ½ inch beyond edge of plate. Fold under extra pastry; crimp edge high. *Do not prick pastry.* ▼ **For filling,** add brown sugar, orange peel, cinnamon, nutmeg, and ginger to potatoes. Stir in eggs and half-and-half. Place pastry shell on oven rack; pour in filling. Cover edge of pie with foil. Bake in a 375° oven 30 minutes. Remove foil. Sprinkle with Hazelnut Streusel Topper. Bake 20 to 25 minutes more or till a knife inserted near the center comes out clean. Cool.

Cornmeal Pastry

In a bowl mix ¾ cup *all-purpose flour*, ½ cup *yellow cornmeal*, 1 tablespoon *sugar*, and ¼ teaspoon *salt*. Using a pastry blender, cut in ⅓ cup *shortening or lard* till pieces are the size of small peas. Sprinkle 3 to 5 tablespoons *cold water*, 1 tablespoon at a time, over mixture, tossing with a fork after each addition till all is moistened. Form into a ball.

Hazelnut Streusel Topper

Mix ¼ cup *all-purpose flour*, ¼ cup *brown sugar*, ⅛ teaspoon *ground cinnamon*, and ⅛ teaspoon ground *nutmeg*. Cut in 2 tablespoons *margarine or butter* till mixture resembles coarse crumbs. Stir in ¼ cup chopped toasted *hazelnuts or almonds*.

SWEET POTATOES

Two-Potato Swirls

Makes 8 servings

Turn holiday stand-bys—sweet potatoes and mashed potatoes—into tempting two-color swirls.

3 large baking potatoes
  (6 to 8 ounces each)
3 large sweet potatoes
  (6 to 8 ounces each)

▼

2 tablespoons margarine *or*
  butter
2 tablespoons milk

▼

2 tablespoons orange juice
1 tablespoon honey

Per Serving

Calories	152
Protein	2 g
Carbohydrate	30 g
Total Fat	3 g
Saturated Fat	1 g
Cholesterol	0 mg
Sodium	45 mg
Potassium	449 mg

Wash, peel, and quarter potatoes. In separate saucepans cook white potatoes and sweet potatoes in a small amount of boiling salted water, covered, for 20 to 25 minutes or till potatoes are tender. Drain. ▼ **In a small mixing bowl** beat hot white potatoes with an electric mixer on low speed till almost smooth. Add *1 tablespoon* of the margarine or butter and the milk. Continue beating till light and fluffy. Transfer to another bowl. ▼ **In the mixing bowl** beat hot sweet potatoes with an electric mixer on low speed till almost smooth. Add remaining 1 tablespoon margarine or butter, the orange juice, and the honey. Continue beating till light and fluffy. ▼ **Line a baking sheet** with foil; spray with nonstick spray coating. Spoon white potato mixture along one side of a decorating bag fitted with a large star tip. Spoon sweet potato mixture along other side of bag. For swirls, on the prepared baking sheet pipe 3-inch circles of the mixture, starting at the outside and working toward the center, building a peak 2 layers high. Make 8 swirls. Cover loosely with plastic wrap; chill till baking time. ▼ **To serve,** bake, uncovered, in a 375° oven for 15 to 20 minutes or till the tips are golden and swirls are heated through. Use a wide spatula to carefully transfer the swirls to dinner plates.

Candied Sweet Potatoes With Apples

Makes 4 servings

Sweet potatoes are not good keepers. Store them in a cool, dry, dark place for up to 1 week.

3 medium sweet potatoes (about 1 pound)
▼
1 large cooking apple
⅓ cup packed brown sugar
1 tablespoon water

1 tablespoon margarine *or* butter
Dash ground cloves
¼ cup chopped pecans *or* walnuts, toasted

Per Serving

Calories	255
Protein	2 g
Carbohydrate	47 g
Total Fat	8 g
Saturated Fat	1 g
Cholesterol	0 mg
Sodium	48 mg
Potassium	448 mg

Wash and peel sweet potatoes. Cut off woody portions and ends. Cut potatoes diagonally into ½-inch-thick slices. ▼ **To steam potato** slices, place the steamer basket in a saucepan. Add water to just below the bottom of the steamer basket. Bring to boiling. Add potato slices. Cover and reduce heat. Steam for 10 to 15 minutes or till just tender. Cool.
▼ **Meanwhile,** core the unpeeled apple and cut into 12 wedges. In a greased two-quart casserole combine potato slices and apple wedges. In a small saucepan bring the brown sugar, water, margarine or butter, and cloves to boiling. Drizzle mixture evenly over potatoes and apples.
▼ **Bake,** uncovered, in a 350° oven for 30 to 35 minutes or till potatoes and apples are glazed, stirring twice. Sprinkle potatoes and apples with toasted pecans or walnuts.

RUTABAGAS

Rutabaga Bake

Makes 4 servings

Per Serving

Calories	343
Protein	10 g
Carbohydrate	36 g
Total Fat	18 g
Saturated Fat	5 g
Cholesterol	16 mg
Sodium	389 mg
Potassium	321mg

1 **pound rutabagas**
▼
¼ **cup milk**
¼ **cup sliced green onion**
1 **tablespoon margarine *or* butter**
2 **teaspoons sugar**
¼ **teaspoon ground ginger**

⅛ **teaspoon pepper**
1 **beaten egg**
▼
¾ **cup soft bread crumbs (1 slice)**
1 **tablespoon margarine *or* butter, melted**
1 **tablespoon snipped parsley**

Refrigerate rutabagas in a plastic bag and they'll last up to 1 month.

Wash and peel rutabagas; cut into ½-inch cubes. (You should have 2¾ cups.) Cook rutabaga, covered, in a small amount of boiling salted water for 30 to 35 minutes or till very tender. Drain well. ▼ **In a large mixing bowl** mash rutabagas with a potato masher or beat with an electric mixer on low speed. Add the milk, green onion, 1 tablespoon margarine or butter, sugar, ginger, and pepper; beat till smooth. Beat in egg. Transfer to a 1-quart casserole. ▼ **In a small mixing bowl** stir together the bread crumbs, 1 tablespoon melted margarine or butter, and parsley. Sprinkle bread crumb mixture over rutabaga mixture. Bake in a 350° oven for 35 to 40 minutes or till top is golden brown.

RUTABAGAS

Rutabaga Remoulade

Makes 4 to 6 servings

Remoulade (*reh moo LAHD*) is a sharp, mayonnaise-based sauce that usually includes anchovy paste. We included the other traditional ingredients, but left out the anchovy paste. If you're a big fan, go ahead and stir a little bit in.

1 **pound rutabagas**

▼

¼ **cup mayonnaise *or* salad dressing**
1 **tablespoon Dijon-style mustard**
1 **tablespoon finely chopped sweet pickle *or* dill pickle**

1 **tablespoon olive oil *or* salad oil**
1 **tablespoon white wine vinegar *or* vinegar**
2 **teaspoons snipped parsley**
½ **teaspoon capers**

Per Serving

Calories	166
Protein	1 g
Carbohydrate	8 g
Total Fat	15 g
Saturated Fat	2 g
Cholesterol	8 mg
Sodium	196 mg
Potassium	285 mg

Wash and peel rutabagas; cut into julienne strips. (You should have about 3 cups). Cook rutabaga, covered, in a small amount of boiling salted water for 18 to 20 minutes or till tender. Drain well. Set aside.

▼ **Meanwhile,** in a medium mixing bowl stir together mayonnaise or salad dressing, mustard, pickle, olive oil or salad oil, vinegar, parsley, and capers. Stir in cooked rutabaga. Toss lightly to coat. Cover and chill for 2 to 24 hours.

PARSNIPS

Curried Parsnips

Makes 4 to 5 servings

Per Serving

Calories	154
Protein	3 g
Carbohydrate	22 g
Total Fat	7 g
Saturated Fat	4 g
Cholesterol	13 mg
Sodium	171 mg
Potassium	442 mg

1 **pound parsnips, cut into ¼- inch-thick slices (2⅔ cups)**

¾ **cup chicken broth**

▼

½ **cup dairy sour cream**

1 **tablespoon all-purpose flour**

1 **to 2 tablespoons snipped fresh cilantro *or* parsley**

½ **teaspoon curry powder**

In a medium saucepan cook parsnips, covered, in boiling chicken broth for 5 to 6 minutes or till tender. *Do not drain.* ▼ **Stir together** sour cream and flour; stir into parsnips along with cilantro or parsley and curry powder. Return to boiling; reduce heat. Cook for 2 minutes more or till heated through. Serve immediately.

If you come home with more parsnips than you can use, refrigerate the remainder in a plastic bag and they'll last up to 10 days.

PARSNIPS

Maple Parsnips

Makes 4 servings

Parsnips are an old-fashioned vegetable with a sweet, nutty flavor. This friendly side dish teams parsnips with their first cousin, the carrot, in a maple syrup-nutmeg glaze.

½ **pound parsnips, cut into ¼-inch-thick slices (1⅓ cups)**

2 **medium carrots, cut into julienne strips (1 cup)**
▼
¼ **cup maple syrup or maple-flavored syrup**

1 **tablespoon margarine or butter**

2 **teaspoons Dijon-style mustard**

¼ **teaspoon ground nutmeg**

⅛ **teaspoon ground cinnamon**

Per Serving

Calories	132
Protein	1 g
Carbohydrate	26 g
Total Fat	3 g
Saturated Fat	1 g
Cholesterol	0 mg
Sodium	144 mg
Potassium	238 mg

In a large saucepan cook parsnips and carrots, covered, in a small amount of boiling salted water for 5 to 7 minutes or till vegetables are tender. Drain well. ▼ **Meanwhile,** for glaze, in a medium saucepan combine maple syrup, margarine or butter, mustard, nutmeg, and cinnamon; bring just to boiling. Stir in cooked parsnips and carrots. Cook about 1 minute or till glazed. Serve immediately.

PARSNIPS

Parsnip Vichyssoise

Makes 4 servings

Per Serving

Calories	210
Protein	5 g
Carbohydrate	21 g
Total Fat	12 g
Saturated Fat	6 g
Cholesterol	28 mg
Sodium	401 mg
Potassium	455 mg

1 medium leek, thinly sliced (⅓ cup)
2 cloves garlic, minced
1 tablespoon margarine *or* butter
1 medium potato, peeled and chopped (1 cup)
1 cup chicken broth
¼ teaspoon salt
¼ teaspoon ground cardamom
⅛ teaspoon pepper

½ pound parsnips, chopped (1½ cups)
▼
1¼ cups half-and-half, light cream, *or* milk
1 teaspoon finely shredded lemon peel
Snipped fresh chives (optional)
Finely shredded lemon peel (optional)

A vichyssoise *(vish ee SWAHZ)* is a chilled, pureed soup that's usually made from potatoes and leeks. Our tasty version includes parsnips and a touch of lemon peel.

In a medium saucepan cook leek and garlic in margarine or butter till tender but not brown. Stir in potato, chicken broth, salt, cardamom, and pepper. Bring to boiling; reduce heat. Cover and simmer for 15 minutes. Stir in parsnips. Cover and cook for 5 to 7 minutes more or till parsnips and potatoes are tender. Cool slightly. ▼ **Place parsnip** mixture in a blender container or food processor bowl. Cover and blend or process till smooth. Pour parsnip mixture into a medium mixing bowl. Stir in the half-and-half, light cream, or milk and the 1 teaspoon lemon peel. If necessary, stir in additional half-and-half to make of desired consistency. Cover and chill well before serving. Ladle into soup bowls. Garnish with snipped chives and additional lemon peel, if desired.

Italian Potatoes

Makes 4 servings

Store fresh
potatoes in a
well-ventilated,
dark place
that's cool and
humid, but
not wet.
Potatoes
should keep
for several
weeks. Do
not refrigerate
potatoes
because they
become overly
sweet and
may darken
when cooked.

2 tablespoons snipped
   fresh basil *or* 1 teaspoon
   dried basil, crushed
2 tablespoons olive oil *or*
   cooking oil
1 tablespoon snipped
   parsley

   ▼

3 medium potatoes, thinly
   sliced (3 cups)
1 small green sweet pepper,
   chopped (½ cup)

1 small red sweet pepper,
   chopped (½ cup)
½ cup finely shredded
   asiago *or* Parmesan
   cheese (2 ounces)
Salt
Pepper

   ▼

2 tablespoons chopped
   pitted black olives

Per Serving

Calories	240
Protein	8 g
Carbohydrate	29 g
Total Fat	11 g
Saturated Fat	1 g
Cholesterol	10 mg
Sodium	254 mg
Potassium	522 mg

In a small mixing bowl stir together basil, olive oil or cooking oil, and parsley; set aside. ▼ **In a 1½-quart** casserole layer *1 cup* of the potatoes, *half* the sweet pepper, *2 tablespoons* of cheese, and *half* of the basil mixture. Sprinkle lightly with salt and pepper. Repeat layers. Top with remaining 1 cup of potatoes and sprinkle lightly with salt and pepper.
▼ **Bake,** covered, in a 350° oven about 40 minutes or till potatoes are tender. Sprinkle with the remaining ¼ cup cheese and the olives. Bake, uncovered, for 2 to 3 minutes more or till cheese melts.

POTATOES

Garlic Mashed Potatoes

Makes 4 servings

Per Serving

Calories	231
Protein	8 g
Carbohydrate	28 g
Total Fat	10 g
Saturated Fat	4 g
Cholesterol	16 mg
Sodium	255 mg
Potassium	521 mg

3 **medium potatoes (1 pound)**

2 **cloves garlic**

▼

2 **green onions, thinly sliced (¼ cup)**

2 **tablespoons margarine *or* butter**

½ **cup grated Romano *or* Parmesan cheese (4 ounces)**

⅛ **teaspoon pepper**
Milk

Don't overbeat your mashed potatoes— a lump or two means they're the real thing!

Quarter the unpeeled potatoes. Cook, covered, in a small amount of boiling salted water for 20 to 25 minutes or till tender. Peel the paper-like outer skin off the garlic cloves. Add the whole garlic cloves to the potatoes for the last 15 minutes of cooking. ▼ **Meanwhile,** cook green onion in margarine or butter till tender but not brown. Drain potatoes and garlic; mash potatoes and garlic with a potato masher or beat with an electric mixer on low speed. ▼ **Add** green onion mixture, Romano or Parmesan cheese, and pepper. Gradually beat in enough milk (⅓ to ½ cup) to make potatoes light and fluffy.

POTATOES

Cheesy Potato Skins

Makes 24

If you like munching these at restaurants, you'll love making them at home! You can make the potato skins ahead, then top and bake them just before serving.

6 **medium baking potatoes (2 pounds)**
¼ **cup margarine *or* butter, melted**

▼

⅔ **cup finely chopped red *or* green sweet pepper**
1 **medium onion, chopped (½ cup)**
¼ **cup coarsely chopped pecans**
2 **cloves garlic, minced**

1 **tablespoon olive oil *or* cooking oil**
1 **cup shredded process Gruyère cheese *or* shredded cheddar cheese (4 ounces)**
4 **slices bacon, crisp-cooked, drained, and crumbled**
2 **tablespoons snipped fresh chives**
Potato Skins

Per Serving

Calories	171
Protein	5 g
Carbohydrate	15 g
Total Fat	11 g
Saturated Fat	3 g
Cholesterol	12 mg
Sodium	115 mg
Potassium	273 mg

For potato skins, prick baking potatoes with a fork. Bake in a 425° oven for 40 to 50 minutes or till tender. Cut into quarters. Scoop out the insides (reserve for another use), leaving ¼-inch-thick shells. Brush both sides of potato skins with melted margarine or butter. Place cut side up on a large baking sheet. Bake in a 425° oven for 10 to 15 minutes or till crisp. ▼ **Meanwhile,** for topping, in a medium saucepan cook the red or green sweet pepper, onion, pecans, and garlic in hot oil till onion is tender but not brown. Remove saucepan from heat and cool slightly. Stir in the cheese, crumbled bacon, and chives. Spoon onto potato skins. Return to oven and bake about 2 minutes or till cheese melts.

French Onion Soup Au Gratin

Makes 4 to 5 servings

Any variety of sweet onion— Walla Walla, Maui, or Vidalia—gives equally delicious results.

2 tablespoons margarine *or* butter
3 medium sweet onions, thinly sliced and separated into rings (2¼ cups)
1 clove garlic, minced
▼
3 cups beef broth
1 cup apple cider *or* apple juice

▼
4 to 6 1-inch-thick slices French bread, toasted
½ cup shredded cheddar cheese
¼ cup grated Parmesan cheese
Cracked black pepper
▼
2 tablespoons snipped fresh chives

Per Serving

Calories	306
Protein	13 g
Carbohydrate	32 g
Total Fat	14 g
Saturated Fat	6 g
Cholesterol	20 mg
Sodium	1,054 mg
Potassium	340 mg

In a large saucepan melt margarine or butter. Stir in onions and garlic. Cook, covered, over low heat about 20 minutes or till onion is very tender and golden, stirring occasionally. ▼ **Stir in** beef broth and apple cider or apple juice. Bring to boiling; reduce heat. Simmer, uncovered, for 10 minutes. ▼ **Meanwhile,** sprinkle each toasted bread slice with a little cheddar cheese, then top each with Parmesan cheese and a little pepper. Place bread on a baking sheet. Broil 4 to 5 inches from heat for 1 to 2 minutes or till cheese melts and turns light brown. ▼ **To serve,** ladle soup into bowls and float bread atop. Sprinkle bread slices with snipped chives.

ONIONS

Baked Onions and Apples

Makes 4 to 5 servings

Per Serving

Calories	343
Protein	10 g
Carbohydrate	36 g
Total Fat	18 g
Saturated Fat	5 g
Cholesterol	16 mg
Sodium	389 mg
Potassium	321 mg

4 **medium sweet onions,
   thinly sliced and
   separated into rings
   (3 cups)**
3 **tablespoons margarine** *or*
   butter

▼

1 **tablespoon all-purpose
   flour**
⅛ **to ¼ teaspoon ground
   cinnamon**
⅛ **teaspoon pepper**
¾ **cup milk**

1 **medium red cooking
   apple, cored and
   coarsely chopped
   (1 cup)**
½ **cup shredded Swiss
   cheese (2 ounces)**

▼

1 **tablespoon margarine** *or*
   butter, softened
4 **to 5 ½-inch-thick slices
   French bread
   Ground cinnamon
   (optional)**

Baked in a
Swiss cheese-
and cinnamon-
flavored sauce,
onions take
on a whole
new life.

In a large skillet cook onions in the 3 tablespoons margarine or butter for 10 minutes or till onions are tender but not brown. Remove onions from skillet, reserving margarine in skillet. Set onions aside.
▼ **In the same skillet** stir in the flour, cinnamon, and pepper. Add milk all at once. Cook and stir over medium heat till thickened and bubbly. Cook and stir for 1 minute more. Return onions to skillet. Stir in chopped apple. Transfer onion mixture to an 8x1½-inch round baking dish. Sprinkle shredded Swiss cheese over onion mixture. ▼ **Spread** the 1 tablespoon softened margarine or butter on *one* side of *each* slice of French bread. Place bread slices, buttered side up, on top of onion mixture. Sprinkle with additional cinnamon, if desired. Bake in a 350° oven for 20 to 25 minutes or till bread is golden.

BRUSSELS SPROUTS

Lemony Brussels Sprouts

Makes 4 servings

Even if you think you don't like brussels sprouts, give this subtle dish a try.

1 pound brussels sprouts (4 cups)

▼

1 tablespoon margarine *or* butter

2 teaspoons lemon juice
¼ teaspoon lemon-pepper seasoning
⅛ teaspoon salt

Per Serving

Calories	63
Protein	2 g
Carbohydrate	8 g
Total Fat	3 g
Saturated Fat	1 g
Cholesterol	0 mg
Sodium	187 mg
Potassium	299 mg

Trim stems and remove any wilted outer leaves from brussels sprouts; wash. Cut sprouts in half lengthwise. ▼ **In a medium saucepan** cook brussels sprouts, covered, in a small amount of boiling salted water for 10 to 12 minutes or till crisp-tender. Drain well. Add margarine or butter, lemon juice, lemon-pepper seasoning, and salt to brussels sprouts; toss gently to coat.

Farmer's Market Tips

Know the market's hours, and get there early for the best selection. Later in the day, there's less to pick from, but you may find reduced prices.

When you arrive, scout out all the vendors' displays to see what's available and to find the best-looking, best-priced produce. Then go back and buy.

Know the produce prices in your local supermarket. That way, you can compare the market's prices to figure out the best deals.

BRUSSELS SPROUTS

Nutty Brussels Sprouts

Makes 4 servings

Per Serving

Calories	100
Protein	4 g
Carbohydrate	12 g
Total Fat	6 g
Saturated Fat	1 g
Cholesterol	0 mg
Sodium	60 mg
Potassium	424 mg

1 **pound brussels sprouts (4 cups)**

▼

1 **tablespoon margarine** *or* **butter**

2 **tablespoons coarsely chopped peanuts**

Salt

Pepper

Don't wash brussels sprouts before storing— just put them in a plastic bag and refrigerate for up to 2 days

Trim stems and remove any wilted outer leaves from brussels sprouts; wash. Cut sprouts in half lengthwise. ▼ **In a medium saucepan** cook brussels sprouts, covered, in a small amount of boiling salted water for 10 to 12 minutes or till crisp-tender. Drain well. Add margarine or butter and toss gently. Place brussels sprouts in a serving bowl. Sprinkle with chopped peanuts. Season to taste with salt and pepper.

Steamed Leeks in Orange Vinaigrette

Makes 4 servings

This simple yet sophisticated side dish pairs well with grilled steaks and some crusty Italian bread.

6 medium leeks (1½ pounds)

▼

2 tablespoons salad oil
½ teaspoon finely shredded orange peel
2 tablespoons orange juice

1½ teaspoons Dijon-style mustard
⅛ teaspoon pepper

▼

1 tablespoon snipped parsley

Per Serving

Calories	143
Protein	2 g
Carbohydrate	19 g
Total Fat	7 g
Saturated Fat	1 g
Cholesterol	0 mg
Sodium	73 mg
Potassium	249 mg

Rinse leeks several times with cold water. Remove any tough outer leaves. Trim roots from base. Cut into ½-inch-thick slices, cutting 1 inch into the green portion. (You should have 2 cups.) ▼ **To steam leek** slices, place a steamer basket in a saucepan. Add water to just below the bottom of the steamer basket. Bring to boiling. Add leeks. Cover and reduce heat. Steam about 5 minutes or till tender. ▼ **Meanwhile,** for orange vinaigrette, in a screw-top jar combine salad oil, orange peel, orange juice, Dijon-style mustard, and pepper. Cover and shake well. ▼ **Pat** leeks dry. Arrange in a shallow dish. Shake vinaigrette well; pour over warm leeks. Cover and let stand at room temperature for 2 to 4 hours. Sprinkle with parsley.

Pork Chops with Leek and Wild Rice Stuffing

Makes 4 main-dish servings

Per Serving

Calories	515
Protein	34 g
Carbohydrate	37 g
Total Fat	24g
Saturated Fat	6 g
Cholesterol	84 mg
Sodium	557 mg
Potassium	749 mg

Refrigerate leeks in a plastic bag for up to 5 days and clean just before using.

5 **medium leeks,**
   (1¼ pounds), thinly
   sliced (1⅔ cups)
1 **clove garlic, minced**
2 **tablespoons margarine** *or*
   butter
1⅔ **cups chicken broth**
⅔ **cup wild rice**
2 **tablespoons finely**
   chopped pecans
2 **tablespoons dry sherry**
1 **teaspoon finely shredded**
   lemon peel

▼

4 **pork rib chops, cut**
   1¼ inches thick
   (about 2 pounds)

▼

1 **medium leek, thinly**
   sliced (⅓ cup)
1 **tablespoon margarine** *or*
   butter
¼ **cup dry white wine** *or*
   water
¼ **cup chicken broth**
1 **teaspoon cornstarch**

For stuffing, in a medium saucepan cook the 1⅔ cups sliced leeks and garlic in the 2 tablespoons margarine or butter till tender. Stir in the 1⅔ cups chicken broth and wild rice. Cover and simmer for 45 to 50 minutes or till rice is tender and liquid is absorbed. Stir in pecans, dry sherry, and lemon peel. ▼ **Meanwhile,** trim fat from chops. Make a pocket in each chop by cutting a horizontal slit from the fat side of the chop almost to the bone. Fill the pocket of each pork chop with stuffing. ▼ **Place stuffed chops** on a rack in a shallow roasting pan. Place any remaining stuffing in a small greased casserole. Bake chops and stuffing, covered, in a 375° oven for 40 to 50 minutes. ▼ **Meanwhile,** for sauce, in a small saucepan cook the ⅓ cup sliced leek in the 1 tablespoon margarine or butter till tender. In a small mixing bowl stir together white wine or water, the ¼ cup chicken broth, and cornstarch. Add wine mixture to saucepan. Cook and stir till thickened and bubbly. Cook and stir for 2 minutes more. Spoon sauce over chops.

Leek and Dried Tomato Appetizer Tart

Makes 16 pieces

Wow your guests with this eye-catching appetizer that doesn't take hours to make. A puff pastry shell holds a creamy ricotta filling loaded with dried tomatoes, leeks, and garlic.

Per Serving

Calories	115
Protein	3 g
Carbohydrate	8 g
Total Fat	7 g
Saturated Fat	1 g
Cholesterol	19 mg
Sodium	102 mg
Potassium	72 mg

½ of a 17¼-ounce package (1 sheet) frozen puff pastry

▼

1 slightly beaten egg white
1 teaspoon water

▼

3 medium leeks (12 ounces)

1 clove garlic, minced
1 tablespoon olive oil *or* cooking oil
¼ cup snipped oil-packed dried tomatoes, drained
Ricotta Filling

Let folded pastry stand at room temperature for 20 minutes to thaw. On a lightly floured surface unfold pastry and roll into a 15x10-inch rectangle. Cut rectangle in half lengthwise. Cut off two ¾-inch-wide strips crosswise, then two ¾-inch-wide strips lengthwise from *each* rectangle. Set the 8 pastry strips aside. ▼ **Place the two rectangles** on an ungreased baking sheet. Combine egg white and water. Brush rectangles with egg white mixture. Place 4 pastry strips on edges of each rectangle to form a border and build up the sides, trimming to fit. Brush strips with egg white mixture. Prick bottom of pastry with a fork. Bake in a 375° oven for 15 minutes. ▼ **Meanwhile,** rinse leeks several times with cold water. Remove any tough outer leaves. Trim roots from base. Cut into ½-inch-thick slices, cutting 1 inch into the green portion. (You should have about 1 cup.) Cook leeks and garlic in hot oil about 5 minutes or till tender. Stir leek mixture and dried tomatoes into Ricotta Filling. Spoon half the filling into each partially baked pastry rectangle. Spread filling to edges. Return to the oven and bake for 10 to 15 minutes more or till edges are golden and filling is set. Bias-slice rectangles crosswise. Serve warm.

Ricotta Filling

In a small mixing bowl combine 1 cup *ricotta cheese,* 1 *egg yolk,* 2 tablespoons *grated Parmesan or Romano cheese,* 1 tablespoon *milk,* and ¼ teaspoon *cracked black pepper.* Stir till smooth.

FENNEL

Fennel Parmigiana
Makes 4 servings

You are probably familiar with the licorice-like taste of fennel seed, which flavors sausages, breads, and cookies. But the less familiar, aromatic parent plant, fennel, offers delicious eating, too. Give it a try in this exquisite side dish.

1 head fennel (about 1 pound)

▼

1 cup water
1 teaspoon instant chicken bouillon granules

▼

2 tablespoons fine dry bread crumbs
1 tablespoon snipped fresh oregano *or* ½ teaspoon dried oregano, crushed

Dash pepper
2 tablespoons margarine *or* butter
2 tablespoons grated Parmesan cheese

▼

¼ cup half-and-half, light cream, *or* milk
2 teaspoons cornstarch
Dash paprika
1 tablespoon dry white wine

Per Serving

Calories	133
Protein	3 g
Carbohydrate	11 g
Total Fat	9 g
Saturated Fat	3 g
Cholesterol	8 mg
Sodium	416 mg
Potassium	392 mg

Cut off and discard upper stalks of fennel. Reserve some of the feathery leaves for garnish. Remove any wilted outer layer of stalks; cut off a thin sliced from fennel base. Wash fennel and cut into quarters lengthwise. ▼ **In a medium saucepan** bring water and bouillon to boiling; add fennel. Cover and simmer about 10 minutes or till tender. ▼ **Meanwhile,** in a small skillet toast bread crumbs, oregano, and pepper in hot margarine or butter. Stir in Parmesan cheese. Drain fennel, reserving ¼ *cup* cooking liquid. ▼ **For sauce,** in the same saucepan combine reserved cooking liquid, half-and-half, light cream, or milk, cornstarch, and paprika. Cook and stir till thickened and bubbly. Cook and stir 2 minutes more. Stir in wine. Spoon sauce over fennel. Top with crumb mixture.

Lamb-Stuffed Fennel

Makes 4 main-dish servings

Per Serving

Calories	241
Protein	20 g
Carbohydrate	15 g
Total Fat	11 g
Saturated Fat	5 g
Cholesterol	116 mg
Sodium	451 mg
Potassium	684 mg

2 **heads fennel (about 2 pounds)**

▼

¾ **pound ground lamb, beef, or pork**
1 **small onion, finely chopped (⅓ cup)**
2 **cloves garlic, minced**
1 **slightly beaten egg**

¼ **cup fine dry bread crumbs**
½ **cup crumbled feta cheese *or* chèvre cheese (2 ounces)**
¼ **teaspoon salt**
¼ **teaspoon pepper**

▼

Leaf lettuce (optional)

A wonderful supper for a snowy winter night.

Cut off and discard upper stalks of fennel. Reserve some of the feathery leaves for garnish. Remove any wilted outer layer of stalks; cut off a thin slice from the base. Wash fennel. Cook fennel, covered, in a small amount of boiling water for 20 to 25 minutes or till tender; drain. Cut the fennel in half lengthwise. Remove center part of fennel, leaving a ½-inch-thick shell; chop and reserve ⅔ cup of the center part of fennel for use in stuffing. Set all aside. ▼ **Meanwhile,** in a large skillet cook ground meat, onion, and garlic till meat is brown and onion is tender. Drain off fat. Stir in the egg, bread crumbs, ¼ *cup* of the cheese, salt, pepper, and reserved chopped fennel. ▼ **Place the fennel** halves in an 8x8x2-inch baking dish. Fill fennel halves with some of the meat mixture; spoon remaining meat mixture around fennel halves in dish. Sprinkle with remaining cheese. ▼ **Bake, covered,** in a 375° oven about 25 minutes or till heated through. If desired, serve on lettuce-lined plates. Garnish with reserved fennel leaves.

FENNEL

Fennel with Red Cabbage

Makes 4 to 6 servings

Pair this colorful side dish with pork, beef, or game.

2 heads fennel (about 2 pounds)
▼
1 clove garlic, minced
2 tablespoons margarine *or* butter
1 cup water
2 tablespoons white vinegar *or* lemon juice
1½ teaspoons instant chicken bouillon granules

¼ teaspoon onion salt
¼ teaspoon white pepper
▼
¼ cup red wine vinegar
¼ cup water
6 cups coarsely shredded red cabbage
▼
4 teaspoons cornstarch
2 tablespoons water

Per Serving

Calories	140
Protein	4 g
Carbohydrate	22g
Total Fat	6 g
Saturated Fat	1 g
Cholesterol	0 mg
Sodium	590 mg
Potassium	886 mg

Cut off and discard upper stalks of fennel. Snip 2 teaspoons of the feathery leaves; reserve remaining tops for garnish. Remove any wilted outer layers of stalks; cut off a thin slice from the base. Wash fennel and cut into quarters lengthwise. ▼ **In a medium saucepan** cook garlic in hot margarine or butter for 1 minute. Add fennel bulbs, the 1 cup water, vinegar or lemon juice, bouillon granules, onion salt, white pepper, and the 2 teaspoons snipped fennel leaves. Bring to boiling; reduce heat. Cover and simmer for 12 to 14 minutes or till fennel wedges are tender.

▼ **Meanwhile,** in a large saucepan bring red wine vinegar and the ¼ cup water to boiling. Add red cabbage. Cover and cook for 8 to 12 minutes or till cabbage is tender. Drain well. Transfer to a serving platter.

▼ **Remove fennel bulbs** from liquid with a slotted spoon; place atop red cabbage. Combine cornstarch and the 2 tablespoons water; add to fennel cooking liquid. Cook and stir till thickened and bubbly. Cook and stir for 2 minutes more. Pour sauce over cabbage and fennel. Garnish with remaining fennel tops.

VEGGIE COMBO

Oven-Roasted Autumn Veggies

Makes 6 servings

An easy, but very tasty way to prepare vegetables.

1 **pound turnips (6 medium), peeled and cut into 1½-inch chunks**
3 **medium potatoes (1 pound), cut into 1-inch pieces**
4 **medium carrots, cut into 1½- inch chunks**
1 **large onion, cut into chunks**
⅓ **cup melted margarine *or* butter**
¼ **cup water**
1 **tablespoon snipped fresh basil *or* 1 teaspoon dried basil, crushed**

1 **tablespoon snipped fresh thyme *or* ½ teaspoon dried thyme, crushed**
½ **teaspoon finely shredded lemon peel**
1 **tablespoon lemon juice**
2 **cloves garlic, minced**
2 **teaspoons salt**
½ **teaspoon cracked black pepper**

▼

½ **cup fine dry bread crumbs**
2 **tablespoons melted margarine *or* butter**

Per Serving

Calories	278
Protein	4 g
Carbohydrate	35 g
Total Fat	15 g
Saturated Fat	2 g
Cholesterol	0 mg
Sodium	1,004 mg
Potassium	579 mg

In a greased 13x9x2-inch baking dish, combine turnips, potatoes, carrots, and onion. In a small mixing bowl combine the ⅓ cup melted margarine or butter, water, basil, thyme, lemon peel, lemon juice, garlic, salt, and pepper. Drizzle over vegetables; toss to coat. Cover and bake in a 350° oven for 45 minutes, stirring once. ▼ **Meanwhile,** in a small mixing bowl combine the bread crumbs and the 2 tablespoons margarine or butter. Sprinkle crumbs over vegetables. Continue baking, uncovered, about 15 minutes more or till vegetables are tender and crumbs are golden.

VEGGIE COMBO

Squash, Pear, and Onion Au Gratin

Makes 6 servings

A scrumptious combination of fall flavors.

Per Serving

Calories	151
Protein	3 g
Carbohydrate	20 g
Total Fat	8 g
Saturated Fat	2 g
Cholesterol	4 mg
Sodium	226 mg
Potassium	391 mg

1½ pounds butternut, butter-cup, *or* banana squash
▼
1 large onion, sliced and separated into rings (1 cup)
1 tablespoon margarine *or* butter
▼
1 medium pear, peeled, cored, and thinly sliced (1 cup)
Salt

▼
3 tablespoons fine dry bread crumbs
3 slices bacon, crisp-cooked, drained, and crumbled
2 tablespoons chopped walnuts
1 tablespoon grated Romano cheese
1 tablespoon melted margarine *or* butter
2 tablespoons snipped parsley

If using butternut squash, cut the squash in half lengthwise. Remove seeds from squash. Peel and slice squash crosswise into ½-inch-thick slices. Set aside. ▼ **Cook onion rings** in 1 tablespoon hot margarine or butter for 5 to 10 minutes or till tender. ▼ **Arrange** *half* of the squash slices in the bottom an 8x8x2-inch baking dish. Top with *half* of the pear slices. Repeat layers. Sprinkle lightly with salt. Cover with cooked onions. ▼ **Bake,** covered, in a 350° oven for 45 minutes or till nearly tender. Meanwhile, in a small mixing bowl combine breadcrumbs, bacon, nuts, cheese, and melted margarine or butter. Sprinkle over vegetables. Bake, uncovered, about 15 minutes more or till squash is tender. Garnish with parsley.

WILD RICE

Wild rice grows wild in Minnesota lakes, so if you live in the "land of 10,000 lakes", you can probably go to a local farmer's market and buy wild rice that's been harvested by hand.

Wild rice is the long, dark brown or black, nutty-flavored seed of an annual marsh grass. Though early explorers dubbed it "rice" because it grows in water, it is not a rice at all and is the only cereal grain native to North America.

Uncooked wild rice keeps indefinitely stored in a cool, dry place or in the refrigerator. If cooked with no added ingredients, you can freeze it for seversl months. It's often combined with brown or white rice and used in cold salads, pilafs, or stuffings.

Wild Rice and Cranberry Pilaf

Makes 6 servings

¾ **cup wild rice**
3 **cups chicken broth**
½ **cup pearl barley**
¼ **cup snipped dried cranberries, apricots, *or* cherries**

¼ **cup dried currants**
1 **tablespoon margarine *or* butter**

▼

⅓ **cup sliced almonds, toasted**

Per Serving

Calories	237
Protein	9 g
Carbohydrate	37 g
Total Fat	7 g
Saturated Fat	1 g
Cholesterol	0 mg
Sodium	416 mg
Potassium	370 mg

Rinse wild rice with cold water; drain. In a saucepan combine rice and chicken broth. Bring to boiling; reduce heat. Cover and simmer for 10 minutes. Remove from heat. Stir in barley, cranberries, apricots, or cherries, currants, and margarine or butter. Spoon into a 1½-quart casserole.

▼ **Bake,** covered, in a 325° oven for 55 to 60 minutes or till rice and barley are tender and liquid is absorbed, stirring once. Fluff rice mixture with a fork; stir in almonds.

Cooking Fresh Vegetables
In the Microwave

Vegetable And Amount	Preparation	Microwave Cooking Directions
Artichokes Two 10-ounce	Wash; trim stems. Cut off 1 inch from tops, and snip off sharp leaf tips. Brush cut edges with lemon juice.	Place in casserole with 2 tablespoons water. Cook, covered, on 100% power (high) for 7 to 9 minutes or till a leaf pulls out easily, rearranging artichokes once. Drain.
Asparagus 1 pound (1½ cups pieces)	Wash; scrape off scales. Break off woody bases where spears snap easily. Leave spears whole or cut spears into 1-inch pieces.	Place in baking dish with 2 tablespoons water. Cook spears or pieces, covered, on 100% power (high) for 7 to 10 minutes or till crisp-tender, rearranging or stirring once.
Beans: green, Italian green, purple, and yellow wax ¾ pound (2¼ cups pieces)	Wash; remove ends and strings. Leave whole or cut into 1-inch pieces. For French-style beans, slice lengthwise.	Place in a casserole with 2 tablespoons water. Cook, covered, on 100% power (high) for 13 to 15 minutes for whole or cut beans (12 to 14 minutes for French-style beans) or till tender, stirring once.
Beets 1 pound (2¾ cups cubes)	For whole beets, cut off all but 1 inch of stems and roots; wash. Do not peel. (For cooking, prick the skins of whole beets.) Or, peel beets; cube or slice.	Place in a casserole with 2 tablespoons water. Cook whole, cubed, or sliced beets, covered, on 100% power (high) for 4 to 7 minutes or till crisp-tender, rearranging or stirring once.
Broccoli ¾ pound (3 cups flowerets)	Wash; remove outer leaves and tough parts of stalks. Cut lengthwise into spears or cut into ½-inch flowerets.	Place in a baking dish with 2 tablespoons water. Cook, covered, on 100% power (high) for 4 to 7 minutes or till crisp-tender, rearranging or stirring once.
Brussels sprouts ¾ pound (3 cups)	Trim stems and remove any wilted outer leaves; wash. Cut large sprouts in half lengthwise.	Place in a baking dish or casserole with 2 tablespoons water. Cook, covered, on 100% power (high) for 4 to 6 minutes or till crisp-tender, stirring once.
Cabbage Half of a 1-to 1¼ pound head (4 cups pieces)	Remove wilted outer leaves; wash. Cut into 4 wedges or cut into 1-inch pieces.	Place in a baking dish or casserole with 2 tablespoons water. Cook, covered, on 100% power (high) for 9 to 11 minutes for wedges (4 to 6 minutes for pieces) or till crisp-tender, rearranging or stirring once.
Carrots 1 pound (3 cups slices)	Wash, trim, and peel or scrub. Cut into ¼-inch-thick slices or julienne strips.	Place in a casserole with 2 tablespoons water. Cook, covered, on 100% power (high) for 7 to 10 minutes for slices (5 to 7 minutes for julienne strips) or till crisp-tender, stirring once.
Cauliflower One 1½-pound head (3 cups flowerets)	Wash; remove leaves and woody stem. Leave whole or break into flowerets.	Place in a casserole with 2 tablespoons water. Cook, covered, on 100% power (high) for 9 to 11 minutes for head (7 to 10 minutes for flowerets) or till tender. Turn, rearrange, or stir once.

Cooking Fresh Vegetables
In the Microwave

Vegetable And Amount	Preparation	Microwave Cooking Directions
Corn 2 cups	Remove husks from fresh ears of corn; scrub with a stiff brush to remove silks. Rinse. Cut kernels from cob.	Place in a casserole with 2 tablespoons water. Cook, covered, on 100% power (high) for 5 to 6 minutes, stirring once.
Corn on the Cob (1 ear equals 1 serving)	Remove the husks from fresh ears of corn; scrub with a stiff brush to remove silks. Rinse.	Wrap each ear in waxed paper; place on microwave-safe paper towels in the microwave. Cook on 100% power (high) for 3 to 5 minutes for 1 ear, 5 to 7 minutes for 2 ears, or 9 to 12 minutes for 4 ears, rearranging once.
Eggplant 1 medium (1 pound) (5 cups cubes)	Wash and peel. Cut into ¾-inch cubes.	Place in a casserole with 2 tablespoons water. Cook, covered, on 100% power (high) for 6 to 8 minutes or till tender, stirring once.ears; rearrange once.
Fennel 2 heads (2½ cups quarters)	Cut off and discard upper stalks, including feathery leaves (reserve leaves for garnish, if desired). Remove wilted outer layer of stalks; cut off a thin slice from base. Wash. Cut fennel into quarters lengthwise.	Place in a casserole with ¼ cup water. Cook covered, on 100% power (high) for 4 to 6 minutes or till tender, rearranging once.
Kohlrabi 1 pound (3 cups julienne strips)	Cut off leaves; wash. Peel; chop or cut into julienne strips.	Place in a casserole with 2 tablespoons water. Cook, covered, on 100% power (high) for 6 to 8 minutes or till tender, stirring once.
Leeks 1½ pounds (3 cups sliced)	Wash well; remove any tough outer leaves. Trim roots from base. Slit lengthwise and wash well. Cut into ½-inch-thick slices.	Place in a casserole with 2 tablespoons water. Cook, covered, on 100% power (high) for 4 to 5 minutes or till tender, stirring once.
Okra ½ pound	Wash; cut off stems. Leave whole or cut into ½-inch-thick slices.	Place in a casserole with 2 tablespoons water. Cook, covered, on 100% power (high) for 4 to 6 minutes or till tender, stirring once.
Onions 1 large (1 cup chopped)	Peel and chop.	Place in a casserole with 2 tablespoons water, margarine, or butter. Cook, covered on 100% power (high) for 3 to 4 minutes or till tender, stirring once.
Parsnips ¾ pound (2 cups slices)	Wash, trim, and peel or scrub. Cut into ¼-inch-thick slices.	Place in a casserole with 2 tablespoons water. Cook, covered, on 100% power (high) for 4 to 6 minutes or till tender, stirring once.
Pea pods ½ pound (2 cups)	Remove tips and strings; wash.	Place in a casserole with 2 tablespoons water. Cook, covered, on 100% power (high) for 3 to 5 minutes or till crisp-tender, stirring once.

Vegetable And Amount	Preparation	Microwave Cooking Directions
Peas, green 2 pounds (3 cups shelled)	Shell and wash. Remove stems.	Place in a casserole with 2 tablespoons water. Cook, covered, on 100% power (high) for 6 to 8 minutes or till crisp-tender, stirring once.
Sweet Peppers: 2 large (2½ cups rings or strips)	Wash and remove seeds and ribs. Cut into rings or strips.	Place strips or rings in a casserole with 2 tablespoons water. Cook, covered, on 100% power (high) for 5 to 6 minutes or till crisp-tender, stirring once.
Potatoes 1 pound (2¾ cups cubes)	Wash and peel. Remove eyes, sprouts, or green areas. Cut into quarters or cube.	Place in a casserole with 2 tablespoons water. Cook, covered, on 100% power (high) for 8 to 10 minutes or till tender, stirring once.
Spinach 1 pound (12 cups torn)	Wash and drain; remove stems.	Place in a casserole with 2 tablespoons water. Cook, covered, on 100% power (high) for 4 to 6 minutes or till tender, stirring once.
Squash: acorn, delicata, golden nugget, and sweet dumpling 1 pound (2 servings)	Wash, halve, and remove seeds.	Place squash halves, cut side down, in a baking dish with 2 tablespoons water. Cook, covered, on 100% power (high) for 6 to 9 minutes or till tender, rearranging once. Let stand, covered, 5 minutes.
Squash: banana, buttercup, butternut, Hubbard, and turban One 1½-pound or a 1½-pound piece	Wash, halve whole squash lengthwise, and remove seeds.	Place squash, cut side down, in a baking dish with 2 tablespoons water. Cook, covered, on 100% power (high) for 9 to 12 minutes or till tender, rearranging once.
Squash: pattypan, yellow, zucchini ¾ pound (2½ cups slices)	Wash; do not peel. Cut off ends. Cut into ¼-inch-thick slices.	Place in a casserole with 2 tablespoons water. Cook, covered, on 100% power (high) for 4 to 5 minutes or till tender, stirring twice.
Sweet potatoes 1 pound	Wash and peel. Cut off woody portions and ends. Cut into quarters.	Place in a casserole with ½ cup water. Cook, covered, on 100% power (high) for 10 to 13 minutes or till tender, stirring once.
Turnips 1 pound (2 ½ cups cubes)	Wash and peel. Cut into ½-inch cubes or julienne strips.	Place in a casserole with 2 tablespoons water. Cook, covered, on 100 % power (high) for 12 to 14 minutes or till tender, stirring once.

Metric Cooking Hints

By making a few conversions, cooks in Australia, Canada, and the United Kingdom can use the recipes in Better Homes and Gardens *Farmer's Market Cookbook* with confidence. The charts on this page provide a guide for converting measurements from the U.S. customary system, which is used throughout this book, to the imperial and metric systems. There also is a conversion table for oven temperatures to accommodate the differences in oven calibrations.

Volume and Weight: Americans traditionally use *cup* measures for liquid and solid ingredients. The chart (bottom right) shows the approximate imperial and metric equivalents. If you are accustomed to weighing solid ingredients, here are some helpful approximate equivalents.
▼ 1 cup butter, caster sugar, or rice = 8 ounces = about 250 grams
▼ 1 cup flour = 4 ounces = about 125 grams
▼ 1 cup icing sugar = 5 ounces = about 150 grams
 Spoon measures are used for smaller amounts of ingredients. Although the size of the tablespoon varies slightly among countries. However, for practical purposes and for recipes in this book, a straight substitution is all that's necessary.
 Measurements made using cups or spoons should always be level, unless stated otherwise.

Product Differences: Most of the ingredients called for in the recipes in this book are available in English-speaking countries. However, some are known by different names. Here are some common American ingredients and their possible counterparts:
▼ Sugar is granulated or caster sugar.
▼ Powdered sugar is icing sugar.
▼ All-purpose flour is plain household flour or white flour. When self-rising flour is used in place of all-purpose flour in a recipe that calls for leavening, omit the leavening agent (baking soda or baking powder) and salt.
▼ Light corn syrup is golden syrup.
▼ Cornstarch is cornflour.
▼ Baking soda is bicarbonate of soda.
▼ Vanilla is vanilla essence.

Oven Temperature Equivalents

Fahrenheit Setting	Celsius Setting*	Gas Setting
300°F	150°C	Gas Mark 2
325°F	160°C	Gas Mark 3
350°F	180°C	Gas Mark 4
375°F	190°C	Gas Mark 5
400°F	200°C	Gas Mark 6
425°F	220°C	Gas Mark 7
450°F	230°C	Gas Mark 8
Broil		Grill

*Electric and gas ovens may be calibrated using Celsius. However, increase the Celsius setting 10 to 20 degrees when cooking above 160°C with an electric oven. For convection or forced-air ovens (gas or electric), lower the temperature setting 10°C when cooking at all heat levels.

Baking Pan Sizes

American	Metric
8x1½-round baking pan	20x4-centimetre sandwich or cake tin
9x1½-inch round baking pan	23x3.5-centimetre sandwich or cake tin
11x7x1½-inch baking pan	28x18x4-centimetre baking pan
13x9x2-inch baking pan	32.5x23x5-centimetre bakingpan
12x7½x2-inch baking dish	30x19x5-centimetre baking pan
15x10x2-inch baking pan	38x25.5x2.5-centimetre baking pan (Swiss roll tin)
9-inch pie plate	22x4- or 23x4-centimetre pie plate
7- or 8-inch springform pan	18- or 20-centimetre springform or loose-bottom cake tin
9x5x3-inch loaf pan	23x13x6-centimetre or 2-pound narrow loaf pan or paté tin
1½-quart casserole 2-quart casserole	1.5-litre casserole 2-litre casserole

Useful Equivalents

¼ cup = 2 fluid ounces = 50ml	
⅓ cup = 3 fluid ounces = 75ml	
½ cup = 4 fluid ounces = 125ml	
⅔ cup = 5 fluid ounces = 150ml	
¾ cup = 6 fluid ounces = 175ml	
1 cup = 8 fluid ounces = 250ml	
⅛ teaspoon = 0.5ml	
¼ teaspoon = 1ml	
½ teaspoon = 2ml	
1 teaspoon = 5ml	
2 cups = 1 pint	
2 pints = 1 litre	
½ inch = 1 centimetre	
1 inch = 2 centimetres